HEROES AN]
OF THE SCOTTISH COVENANTERS

A CONVENTICLE IN A HIGHLAND GLEN

Heroes and Heroines of the Scottish Covenanters

J. Meldrum Dryerre

At the risk of their lives with their flocks they would meet
In storm and in tempest, in rain and in sleet;
Where the mist in the moor-glens lay darkest, 'twas there,
In the thick cloud concealed, they assembled for prayer.

In cities, the wells of salvation were sealed,
More brightly to burst in the moor and the field;
And the Spirit which fled from the dwellings of men,
Like a manna-cloud rained round the camp on the glen.

JOHN RITCHIE LTD
CHRISTIAN PUBLICATIONS

40 Beansburn, Kilmarnock, Scotland

ISBN-13: 978 1 907731 50 1

www.ritchiechristianmedia.co.uk

Typeset by John Ritchie Ltd., Kilmarnock
Printed by Bell & Bain Ltd., Glasgow

PREFACE.

THE story of the Covenanting struggle in Scotland grows in interest the more we study it. The Covenanters were right noble men and women, fired by a holy purpose, free from all selfish aims, with a terribly grand sense of duty, and willing to endure all privations for what they knew to be right. " If you knew them, you would love them ; they are a Godly lot," said Cromwell, writing about his Ironsides. The same can be said of the Covenanters.

A book like this needs no apology for its existence. Each age has told the story of the Covenanting movement. Some of the books thus written are classics on the subject. Their language and style have, however, long since made them unpopular. It is the aim of this small volume to lay before the busy reader of to-day, in simple words, The Covenanters' Story.

It may claim some merit in bringing, within the compass of one hundred and sixty pages, not only what the men did, but what the women suffered.

The deeper study of history has done much to restore interest in the aspirations of these seventeenth-century heroes and heroines. They have long unjustly suffered from uncritical and partisan historians.

The love for the Stuart dynasty died hard in Scotland. So long as there was a Pretender, the Covenanters could expect nothing but contumely. Yet the Stuarts had no warmer or sincerer friends than these men, whom they despised and murdered. With the death of the prejudice in favour of the Stuart line, the hour has come for a dispassionate estimate of the worth and aspirations of the Covenanters. In a humble way, this is attempted in this book. We are confident the hour is nigh when these despised "hill-folk" will receive the honour and esteem they deserve.

There is need to repeatedly remind ourselves that our liberty and its privileges were bought with a great price for us. We are the heirs of the ages. The blood of heroic men and women in the past has watered the ground from which springs our abundant harvest to-day. The age in which we live tends to self-interest. We need to be aroused to perform our duty in the hour that is. No one can read about the Covenanters without being inspired to live a nobler life. We trust that this little volume may not only help in this direction, but that it may be instrumental in leading the young men and maidens of our land to be equally heroic in faithfully fulfilling their duty in the positions of life to which they are called. The need of heroes and heroines is still as urgent as ever. The opportunity of being such is found in the common walks of life. The conditions are altered, but the struggle is none the less real.   J. M. D.

CONTENTS

CHAPTER   PAGE

I. INTRODUCTION -   -   -   -   -   -   9

II. THE MARQUIS OF ARGYLE   -   -   -   24

III. REV. JAMES GUTHRIE   -   -   -   -   36

IV. REV. HUGH M'KAIL -   -   -   -   -   46

V. REV. DONALD CARGILL   -   -   -   -   56

VI. THE WIGTON MARTYRS   -   -   -   -   71

VII. RICHARD CAMERON -   -   -   -   -   84

VIII. FAITHFUL UNTO DEATH   -   -   -   92

IX. ALEXANDER PEDEN, THE PROPHET -   -   99

X. JAMES RENWICK   -   -   -   -   -   108

XI. SOME HEROINES OF THE COVENANT -   -   124

XII. THE BAILLIES OF JERVISWOODE   -   -   139

XIII. LADY CALDWELL   -   -   -   -   -   149

XIV. SOME WONDERFUL ESCAPES   -   -   -   152

HEROES AND HEROINES

SCOTTISH COVENANTERS.

I.

INTRODUCTION.

Aim of Writer.—In the next few pages it will be
our aim to lay before the reader a short history of the
Covenanting struggle. It is our hope to make this
popular and brief, rather than tedious and exhaustive.
We will only slightly touch some unimportant periods
in our history, therefore, and may treat generously some
periods that are generally considered important. Whatever is done will be found fair to all parties, and resting
on the researches of our best historians.

Need of an Introduction.—There is all the more
need for a statement of the principles that actuated the
Covenanters, as it is difficult to remove from the public
mind the false ideas put there by the illustrious Sir
Walter Scott in his *Tales of a Grandfather.* It has
been too common to make fun of the peculiarities of

speech: to exaggerate the follies of one or two leaders
in the movement: and to attribute to them motives
not the highest; rather than sympathetically learn their
thoughts and feelings. They have been treated too often
as fanatics and rebels: the age, however, is redeeming
their good name and ranking them with the heroes
and heroines who have been the glory of Scotland.

It is not to be supposed that men gave up their
estates and became wanderers on the face of the earth,
enduring all the horrors of living in damp caves and
amidst treacherous moss-hags, and giving up their life
for their faith, unless their hearts and minds were deeply
moved by strong principles. The Covenanters believed
their present and eternal welfare was at stake. To give
up the Covenants was to give up God. And the very
principles that they fought and bled for are recognised
as of supreme worth to-day. If the Covenanters require
defence, they find it in the Revolution of 1688. What
was done then, the Covenanters tried to do fifty years
earlier.

Genesis of the Covenanting Struggle.—With the
opening of the sixteenth century, we find Europe beginning to awake from the moral stupor that had so long
enthralled her. For this moral imbecility Rome was
to blame. She had kept her children within her grasp
by an appeal to superstition, which was fostered by
ignorance. The Bible had arisen, and its light was
hurling back the darkness of ignorance, and giving life
where before there was death.

Linked with the " death-hand " of the Romish Church,
and supported by it, was the absolutism of our kings. The
liberty of the subject was but then in swaddling clothes,

with its life threatened on every side. But the Bible was good food to feed upon, and if only the Scriptures once managed to get scattered broadcast, the child would grow strong.

As far as absolutism is concerned, it declined little in power during the reign of Henry VIII. But it was when he defied Rome that religious freedom made great progress. It cannot be said there was much virtue in the heart of Henry in the step he took; bu⁺ a king's folly is often for the blessing of the nations.

Scotland was not slow to pay her part of th price of religious and civil liberty. As early as the beginning of the fifteenth century she had welcomed a company of persecuted Wycliffites into her midst, and the men and women of Ayrshire, Perthshire, and Fifeshire had gladly listened to the preaching of the gospel. Attempts were made to suppress these preachers, and a number were killed, but others were ever ready to take their place.

It was the martyrdom of Wishart, however, that opened the eyes of the people thoroughly to the aims of Rome, and allowed them to see the wretched plight they were in. How much John Knox owed to Wishart will never be fully known. This can readily be allowed, however —the martyrdom provoked in Knox the keenest hostility to Romanism, a Church that could so cruelly murder such a gentle and learned spirit as Wishart.

It is no surprise, therefore, to find in the days of **Knox** that men here and there joined themselves into bands and covenanted together. The chief feature of these early covenants is, that the fear of Rome's power is found in each covenant. "We covenant to refuse all company with idolatry." "We vow, by the **grace** of

God, that we shall with all diligence apply the whole
power, substance, and our very lives to maintain, set
forward, and establish the most blessed Word of God."
The "Confession of Faith" drawn up by Knox and
others was a covenant which Parliament endorsed.
The hour of triumph came when, in 1592, the Parliament
passed an Act entitled "Ratification of the Liberties of
the True Church." As the Covenanting struggle had as
its main object the upholding of the liberties this Act
ratified, we will summarise its chief articles.

The Kirk demanded from her members that until death
they must maintain that the State has no control over the
spiritual affairs of the Kirk; that Jesus Christ is King of
the Kirk, and whoever tries to usurp His place must be
resisted; that bishops are not of New Testament origin,
and that all ministers are of equal rank; that no man
can be a priest to dispense grace to men, but *all* are
priests.

With such principles put as the very life of their
religion, it is easy to see that Rome and the King must
sooner or later try to crush the Kirk.

The Crisis in the Struggle.—Although we have
traced the symptoms of the Covenanting struggle back
to the general struggle in Europe for light and liberty,
yet the acute crisis came to the Covenanters when
Charles I. ascended the throne. In many ways Charles
was better than his father, but in one he was his equal—
he hated the black bread of Presbyterianism, and declared
it no fit religion for a gentleman. Episcopacy, because
it preached the Divine Right of Kings, he loved, and
determined to force it upon the Scottish people, despite
all his vows to uphold Presbyterianism. He accordingly

began to undermine the strength of the Covenanting nobles by taking from them their State positions, and conferring them upon Episcopalians. He added to this by demanding all the Church lands the nobles had acquired when Romanism was abolished, to enable him to pay his Episcopalian clergy, and also to add to his own exchequer.

Because these acts caused little apparent discontent, Charles next introduced, on his own authority, *The Book of Canons*. This was a direct blow at the Kirk, and to the ruin of Charles, the Covenanters took the matter quietly. The moment, however, his Liturgy, with its Romish conceits, was introduced, the dark thunder-cloud burst. Each man looked at the other, trying to discover a leader in the great crisis that had come. Men from all parts of the country hurried to Edinburgh. Determination was written upon their faces as they entered Greyfriars' Churchyard. When the National Covenant was read over, and the Earl of Sutherland had signed it, a long sigh of relief came from the excited multitude, and men opened their veins and signed it with their blood. Within two months the whole nation had practically signed the Covenant, and Charles found himself confronted with an army of 30,000 men led by General Leslie. They easily conquered Charles, and apparently Romanism was destroyed and the liberty of the subject guaranteed.

A time of Declension.—After their victory over Charles they took the side of the English Independents, and English liberty was assured at Marston Moor. But clan blood is strong in Scotland, and the moment Cromwell had humbled Charles, the Scottish heart was filled

with pity. Some undoubtedly believed in the trust-
worthiness of Charles, which will account for what they
did. Under the Marquis of Hamilton a section of the
Covenanters made " An Engagement " with Charles. For
the upholding of their privileges they agreed to enter
England and fight Cromwell. The battle of Preston,
however, scattered this army.

It was now the opportunity for the strict Covenanters
to enter into power under the leadership of the Marquis
of Argyle. He had no faith in Charles, and believed it
suicidal for the Covenanters to enter into treaty with
the King. He therefore got passed in Parliament the
celebrated " Act of Classes," which aimed at punishing
all who had agreed to the " Engagement " made by the
Marquis of Hamilton, by debarring these men from
holding State appointments. Some, however, protested
against this severity, and the Covenanting party was
further divided. The cementing bond, however, was the
execution of Charles I. Both parties of Covenanters
agreed in crowning Charles II. at Scone, when the
Marquis of Argyle carried the crown. The oath that
Charles took filled the Covenanters with joy. " I,
Charles, King of Great Britain, France, and Ireland, do
assure and declare, by my solemn oath in the presence
of Almighty God, the searcher of hearts, my allowance
and approbation of the National Covenant and the
Solemn League and Covenant." But the defeat at
Worcester in 1651 not only crushed Royalism, but
seemed to have destroyed the Covenanters.

The Restoration Persecution.—The hour of the
Restoration was not a happy one for the Covenanters, for
it was their standing by the English Independents that

"PREACHING IN THE VALLEYS."

crushed Charles I. and led to his death. Charles II. was not slow to let Scotland see that Presbyterianism was obnoxious to him—that he firmly believed in the Divine Right of Kings. He picked for his work two suitable men, Middleton, whom he made King's Commissioner, and Sharp, who became Archbishop of St Andrews.

When these two men were let loose a reign of terror commenced in Scotland. Public meetings were forbidden, books were condemned, speeches against the King or the Government were punished. The Divine Right of Kings had to be accepted on oath ; those who refused were charged with treason. Episcopacy was established in 1662, when the following Declaration was passed in Parliament:—" That the ordering and disposal of the external government and policy of the Church doth properly belong unto His Majesty, as an inherent right of the crown, by virtue of his royal pre rogative and supremacy in causes ecclesiastical." All the ministers were accordingly called to the bishops' meetings and threatened with punishment if they declined assent to this Declaration. Rather than violate their conscience 400 ministers left their manses and churches in the middle of winter. Middleton was amazed at the sight, and asked in derision, " What *will* these mad fellows do ? " Sharp soon declared what he would do to these godly ministers. They were prohibited from preaching under the penalty of death. And all who went to their meetings were threatened with death. And now that the Government had beheaded the Marquis of Argyle there was no one to lead the Covenanters, and they were being torn to pieces by the soldiers who were scattered all over the land.

The Fight for Freedom.—It required very little to make the Covenanters take up arms against the oppressors. In November 1666 the Covenanters were hiding in the hilly part of Glenkens. Coming down to Dalry for food they found that some soldiers of Sir James Turner's troop were stationed there. They met the soldiers driving several people to thrash the corn of an old man who had been fined for not attending church. The Covenanters did not interfere, but next morning they heard that the soldiers had laid hold of the old man and were about to roast him. They hurried to the old man's house and found him lying bound on the floor.

" Why do you bind the old man ? "

" How dare you challenge us ? " replied the soldiers. Whereupon the Covenanters went forward to release the man, and the soldiers drew upon them. A fight ensued and the soldiers were taken prisoners. Now that they had taken this step another had to be taken. The remainder of the soldiers at Balmaclellan must be disarmed. This accomplished, other Covenanters joined them. Marching quietly, they entered Dumfries and took Sir James Turner prisoner. Their army grew larger each day and they prepared for resistance. This was the resolution they passed.

" That they were in the way of their duty, and if their design failed they could say, it was in their heart to build a house to the Lord, and to act for the glory of God and the cause of religion and liberty, for which they were willing to die as sacrifices ; and they reckoned a testimony for the Lord and their country was a sufficient reward for labour, loss, and death."

They moved on to the Pentlands, and at Rullion

Green were defeated with much loss ; and the prisoners were treated with great severity, some being executed after great torture.

Indulgence and its Result.—The defeat of the Pentland rising was followed by a period of quietness, owing to saner counsels being followed in the Government of the country. Only one of two courses was now possible : either to crush the Covenanters with greater severity, or to relax the restrictions in the matter of religious worship. After a considerable lapse of time the latter was adopted, and the Government offered what was called "*An Indulgence.*" By this the King, in June 1669, allowed those ministers who had left their churches rather than agree to Episcopalianism to return on certain conditions. They were to get the manse and glebe, but no stipend ; they were not allowed to preach in any parish but their own ; and no one was allowed to attend the ordinances from any other parish.

All who agreed to be ordained by the bishops were restored to full privileges. The effect of this Indulgence was to cause further friction. The Government constantly interfered with the ministers, charging them with doing things that were unlawful. Besides, all those who agreed to accept the benefits of the Indulgence were continually disagreeing with those who refused to acknowledge the humiliating conditions laid upon the gospel. And to crown all, the Government broke out in great fury against the non-Indulged, and the last persecution was worse than the first.

When Lord Lauderdale allowed Lord Rothes, Archbishop Sharp, and Lord Halton to have the Government of Scotland practically in their hands the persecution was renewed in right earnest. Severe laws were passed against the Covenanters. The outed ministers were only allowed to preach and pray in their own houses, under the penalty of imprisonment and fine for disobedience. Persons who attended such meetings were to be fined according to their station in life. Masters were made responsible for their servants.

And when they came to deal with the hill-meetings they were not less severe. Any preacher found conducting a meeting in a field or on the hill-side was put to death. The person who arrested him received £30, and if by mischance the arrester killed the preacher he was excused. Persons found attending these meetings were fined double those attending meetings indoors. Every man was compelled to go to the church under heavy fines. And when we remember that a large number of the new ministers were ignorant and immoral, drawn from the farms and army, we shall not be surprised that in the county of Renfrew about £90,000 was extracted as fines ; the Marquis of Athole drawing £5000 in one week for his own pocket. Hundreds of men were caught and sold as slaves in Virginia and Barbadoes. Dozens were shot, scores had their noses slit and their ears cut off.

In 1677 no fewer than 17,000 persons were persecuted for the crime of attending the hill-meetings. Soldiers were allowed to run wild all over the country. A host of 10,000 rough warlike Highlanders were brought from the Highlands and allowed to overrun the country as they pleased. Wodrow tells us that " when the Highlanders went back one would have thought they had been at the sacking of some besieged town, by their baggage and luggage. They were loaded with spoil. They carried away a great many horses, and no small quantity of goods out of merchants' shops, whole webs of linen and woollen cloth, some silver plate bearing the names and arms of gentlemen. You would have seen them with loads of bedclothes, carpets, men and women's clothes, pots, pans, shoes, and other furniture whereof they had pillaged the country." The invasion cost Ayr alone £36,000, but nothing was too great as long as the Covenanters were being punished!

But the Covenanters aroused themselves when Hackston and Balfour and others, searching for a cruel sheriff who mercilessly persecuted the Covenanters, to chastise him, met Sharp, the Archbishop of St Andrews, and killed him as the enemy of God.

"I take God to witness," said Balfour, "whose cause I desire to own in adhering to this persecuted gospel, that it is not out of hatred to thy person, nor for any prejudice thou hast done or could do to me that I intend to take thy life this day; but it is because thou hast been, and still continuest to be, an avowed opposer of the flourishing of Christ's Kingdom, and murderer of the saints, whose blood thou hast shed like water on the ground."

To the constitutional mind this crime cannot be defended. We must remember, however, it took place in the seventeenth century, and under great provocation.

The Covenanters now drew closer together, and met armed for fighting. When, therefore, on June 1, 1679, they were disturbed in their conventicle at Avondale by the cry, "The soldiers are coming," Thomas Douglas stopped his sermon and said, "You have got the theory,

now for the practice." And at the swamps of Drumclog
they sang the 76th Psalm, met Claverhouse and his
dragoons and scattered them to the wind. But the vain
success of battle gained them little. Again at Bothwell
Bridge they fought and were defeated, owing largely to
there being too many commanders, jealous of each other's
authority. No quarter was given to those who were
found with weapons. Four hundred were butchered.
Twelve hundred who surrendered were stripped and made
to lie flat on the ground, those being shot who sat up.
The remainder were dragged into Edinburgh and met by
a mob, who cried, " Where's your God ? Where's your
God ? " The prisons were filled, and the Greyfriars'
Churchyard was used for those who could not be stuffed
into the prisons. Two clergymen were executed, Kidd
and King. Over thirty died of disease. Two hundred
and fifty were put on board a vessel at Leith to be taken
out to the American plantations and sold as slaves, but
the vessel was wrecked on the coast of Orkney and 200
were drowned. And Scotland was a bleeding country,
but she still had her 7000 who had not bowed the knee
to Baal.

The Final Stage in the Struggle.—What Cromwell
had declared years before *must* come to pass, and what
the Covenanters had fought him for declaring must come
to pass, they now saw was inevitable—the House of
Stuart must be abolished. Donald Cargill prepared
the Queensferry paper in 1680, which expressed the
feelings of the Covenanters. " We do reject the King and
those associate with him in the Government . . . . from
being our King and rulers . . . . being no more bound
to them, they having altered and destroyed the Lord's

established religion, overturned the fundamental and established laws of the kingdom, taken away altogether Christ's Church Government, and changed the civil Government of this land, which was by a King and a free Parliament, into tyranny. . . . . We bind and oblige ourselves to defend ourselves and one another in our worshipping of God, and in our natural, civil and divine rights and liberties, till we shall overcome, or send them down under debate to posterity, that they may begin where we end."

There is no uncertainty in this, and it breathes what has long been accepted,—the rights of the subject.

Richard Cameron took up the work from the point Cargill left it. He roused the nation by his preaching, and by the "Sanquhar Declaration" he believed he would shake the throne of Britain. Though he did not live to see his prophecy fulfilled, the Revolution of 1688 carried out the terms of his declaration. And in the new settlement that took place when William of Orange came to the throne, the principles which the Covenanters had so zealously fought for all these years were those which formed the integral part of the settlement. And from that day to this, each monarch has to acknowledge these principles before he is allowed to enter into the glory of the throne.

II.

THE MARQUIS OF ARGYLE.

In the early days of the Covenanting struggle two names stand out prominently, the one a minister, James Guthrie, the other a nobleman, the Marquis of Argyle. Of both we are entitled to say, their blood baptised the cause of freedom, of conscience, and pure religion. Their martyrdom proved the vindictiveness of the men who opposed the Covenanters, who became more courageous and determined the more they were persecuted.

From a very early period in Scottish history the house of Argyle played a prominent part. They were the High Justiciars of all Scotland, executing the royal authority both in civil and criminal causes until the Court of Session was instituted, when this power was only exercised over the western part of Scotland. Still this made the Argyles rulers over a multitude of men, who would follow their chief in preference to the King. Indeed, it is stated that the eighth Earl, the subject of this sketch, could have put on the field 20,000 men.

As far as land went, the Argyles have ever been masters of vast domains. From the far north to the Mull of Kintyre and the estuary of the Clyde in length, and at places nearly the whole breadth of Scotland, was included in their domains. Besides, they had estates in the shires of Renfrew, Ayr, Perth, together with large mansions in all the chief towns of Scotland.

When we remember, too, that the eighth Earl received a promise from Charles to repay £150,000 for expenses and disbursements made on the King's behalf, we have some conception of the greatness of the Argyles. It was no wonder, therefore, that when the Earl joined the Covenanters in the General Assembly of 1638, Baillie should say: "No one thing did confirm us so much as Argyle's presence. The man was the far most powerful subject in our kingdom,"—a fact which seems to utterly destroy the charge made against him by his enemies, that he was a Covenanter, not because he loved liberty or religion, but because he hoped to add to his own greatness. Argyle had everything to lose and nothing particular to gain by his adhesion to the Covenanting interest, and we are bound to think about him as a true-hearted and patriotic hero.

Archibald, eighth Earl of Argyle, was born in 1598, and was known as Lord Lorn during his minority. His father was a peculiar man, and had to flee the country for debt, and served the King of Spain in Flanders.

Lord Lorn, deprived of his father, was placed under the care of the Earl of Morton, who gave Lorn an education superior to the majority of men in his day. After the usual course of classics, Lord Lorn studied theology and jurisprudence, no doubt in preparation for the position he expected to fill in the government of his country.

After travelling hither and thither he went to the court of Charles I., and became at once a favourite with his royal master. He was made a Privy Councillor, and

was used by Charles in many important matters connected with the kingdom.

It was during this period that the episode occurred
which has been much used by the detractors of Lord
Lorn. His father returned from abroad, and, joining the
court of Charles, was received graciously, especially as
the father had become a Roman Catholic. He soon
showed a most intense hatred of Lord Lorn, and determined, if possible, to disinherit him. Charles, however,
preferred the son to the father, and immediately ordered
the old Earl to assign to his son the estates and honours
of the house of Argyle, leaving for the father a life
interest in the estate. To this the old Earl assented
after much pressure, but not with good grace.

" I submit to the King's pleasure, though I believe I
am hardly dealt with," he said to the King. He then
turned to Lord Lorn and said, " I have to call to your
remembrance how undutiful your carriage has been
towards me ; but bear ever in mind how bountiful the
King has been to you, which yet I am sure you will
forget." He bowed to the King, and was about to retire.
His anger, however, made him once more address Charles.

" Sire, I know this young man better than you can
do. You have brought me low, that you may raise him.
I doubt you will live to repent. He is a man of craft,
subtlety, and falsehood, and can love no man ; and if
ever he finds it in his power to do you mischief, he will
be sure to do it." A most terrible malediction to come
from a father.

Yet the picture that we have of him in his home,
with his most excellent wife, Margaret, the daughter of
the Earl of Morton, shows how little the father knew

the son. It was the custom of the Earl to rise at five o'clock in the morning, and to continue in private until eight o'clock, and, besides family worship and private prayer in the morning and evening, he usually prayed with his wife at the same seasons, his valet and her maid being present. Their home became the resting place of some of the most godly ministers in the land, and Samuel Rutherford blesses God that He had sent him a friend in my Lord Lorn.

With such a pious wife, and his own heart centred on religious things, it could not be otherwise than that he should sympathise with the Covenanters. Hitherto he had not identified himself with them in their struggle against Popery and Prelacy, and for liberty of person and conscience. As we have seen, he took the decisive step when he attended the General Assembly of 1638, where he was warmly welcomed, and chided for not coming sooner.

" It was not want of affection to the good of religion and my country that detained me, but a desire, a hope that by staying with the court I might have been able to bring about a redress of grievances. And when I saw that I could not stay longer, without proving unfaithful to God and my country, I felt that it behoved me to join myself openly to your society."

The close of this Assembly was the beginning of the preparations for war with Charles, and the Earl of Argyle, who had succeeded to the title on his father's death, was sent to subdue the Western Highlands, which he did. The power of the Covenanters brought Charles to his senses, and, ever ready to give promises, he satisfied the Covenanters, and even went the length to create Argyle a Marquis as a token of his favour.

When the English Parliament had made Charles nothing less than a captive, the sympathy of Scotland awoke. Under the leadership of the Marquis of Hamilton, a movement was started to throw the forces of the Covenanters on to the Royalist side and thus assist Charles against the Independents. It was in this crisis that the Marquis of Argyle showed his wisdom. He opposed the measure fiercely, believing that the Independents were only fighting for that which the Covenanters had fought for, and to assist the King against the Independents was to condemn themselves, and give a King who could not be trusted great power to do evil. A large number of the people took the side of Argyle, and he became the chief man in the nation. Those who had made the *Engagement* with Charles invaded England and were routed at Preston.

Since there was division amongst themselves, caused by continual treating with and then fighting Charles, Argyle brought forward the celebrated " Act of Classes," which was intended to do for Scotland what Cromwell's self-denying ordinance did in England. By this " Act of Classes " all general officers, chief movers, and officials who had made themselves active in the *Engagement* were debarred from taking public office or holding positions of trust. This severity only led to greater divisions however. But these divisions were cemented for a time by the death of Charles I.

The heart of the Marquis of Argyle was filled with great gladness when Charles II. gave signs that he would respect the claims of the Covenanters, and not enforce the Episcopalian religion upon his people.

The coronation ceremony at Scone, on January 1, 1651,

was one of great splendour. Perhaps underneath all the loyalty there was much fear, but it was not shown. The crown was carried by the Marquis of Argyle before the King, and at the proper time placed on the King's head. The sermon preached was an appeal to the King to remember his pledges.

Argyle was deeply anxious that the nation should have rest after its long period of disquiet. He knew that a large number outside did not believe in the King's promises. He therefore suggested to Charles that it would set the mind of the nation at rest if he married into some well-known Presbyterian family. Who it was that suggested the name will never be known, but Charles agreed to marry the daughter of Argyle, Lady Anne. In the same letter he promised Argyle a dukedom, and to repay all monies he had paid out for the King. It may have been that this alliance was to secure himself from his enemies; but we hardly think we are to declare that Argyle was an unprincipled place-seeker, even although we admitted that he might have had visions of getting his family set upon the throne. It was a mistake, how- ever, that cost the reason of Lady Anne, and has ever exposed Argyle to the scorn of his enemies. Charles fulfilled none of his promises.

Soon after this the lewd life of Charles became an eyesore to the Covenanters. No one seemed brave enough to speak to the King but Argyle. The opportunity came at Stirling. After supper he went with the King into his closet, and there with much freedom laid before him the sinfulness of his conduct. Charles seemed to take the rebuke kindly, indeed penitently, for he wept. The Marquis seemed much elated at the reception Charles had given his rebuke, but the Marchioness, with greater insight of character, declared : " He is not to be trusted. You have now the King as your enemy, and he will never forgive you."

ARCHIBALD CAMPBELL, EARL OF ARGYLE.

Apparently, however, Argyle still retained the King's favour, even although he opposed the invading of England by the Scottish army. He therefore remained at Stirling with the Marchioness, who was lying seriously ill. The defeat of Charles showed the wisdom of Argyle.

During the period that elapsed between the battle of Worcester and the Restoration, Argyle was the chief ruler of the Scottish nation. It was a period of extreme difficulty, requiring great tact and wisdom. Argyle, after some pressure, agreed to acknowledge Cromwell, who had been everywhere victorious, as ruler. This acknowledgment was one of the indictments made against Argyle at his trial. He defended himself by saying he could do no other. " It is evident, how clearly and freely I may say, that I do not deserve to be a single sufferer in all His Majesty's dominions for my carriage during the late troubles, His Majesty having pardoned all but some of the murderers of his late royal father. What could I think of that matter, after a man so eminent in the law as His Majesty's Advocate took the engagement to Cromwell ?"

As in the case of Charles I., so in that of Charles II., Argyle had lost all faith in the King's honesty. Religion was to be trampled upon ruthlessly if Charles II. came back to Scotland, and he, therefore, protested against men trying to bring back a man to the throne who was the enemy of God. It was an opinion that required some fortitude to express, and one that might cost him his life if Charles came back ; but it was expressed fearlessly, because he believed in the truth of it.

When Charles II., therefore, was restored to the throne, Argyle went to his Highland home to await the turn of affairs. His son, Lord Lorn, being a Royalist, was with the King. After some time Argyle wrote Charles through Lord Lorn, asking permission to come to London. The

King gave an answer that warranted the Marquis going. He entered Whitehall to salute Charles, who immediately, with an angry stamp of the foot, commanded Sir William Fleming to execute his order, who thereupon conveyed the Marquis to the Tower.

Charles had raised up in Scotland tools, who were ready to do his commands. The Covenanters, who had assisted Cromwell at the crucial hour of English history, which led to Charles I. being beheaded, were to feel the cruelty of his son's anger. Argyle, as the embodiment of the Covenanting spirit, was in his power, and Charles gave explicit directions to Middleton—"Behead the Marquis of Argyle."

On the 16th April 1661, Argyle was brought before the Scottish Parliament charged with treason. The indictment consisted of fourteen heads, the chief of which were: That he had called together the Committee of Estates in 1643; entered into the Solemn League and Covenant with England; protested in Parliament against the Engagement to relieve Charles I. in 1648; raised an army to oppose the Engagers; submitted to Cromwell; and was accessory to, and acquainted with, the design to murder Charles I.

It will be seen that all these are directly connected with, and flow out naturally from, his allegiance to the Covenanting cause. He could do no other and be true to the best interests of liberty and religion. Some of the charges were withdrawn, and others were shown to be not criminal. Indeed, so doubtful was the result of the trial, so well did the Marquis defend himself, that Chancellor Glencairn, Lord Rothes, and Archbishop Sharp posted to London to see what was to be done.

Monk supplied what was needed in the form of private letters. Parliament seemed satisfied, and the Marquis was convicted of treason, and ordered to be beheaded two days later. This would prevent Lord Lorn prevailing with Charles for the life of the Marquis.

" You have the indemnity of an earthly king among your hands, and have denied me a share in that," he said, after his sentence was pronounced, " but you cannot hinder me from the indemnity of the King of kings. Shortly you must be before His tribunal, and I pray He may not mete out such measure to you as you have done to me, when you are called to account for all your acting, and this among the rest. I had the honour to set the crown upon the King's head, and now he hastens me to a better crown than his own."

When he arrived at the prison, the Marchioness, in great distress, awaited him.

" They have given me till Monday to be with you, my dear, therefore let us make for it," he said as he met her.

" The Lord will requite it, the Lord will requite it," she said in a burst of tears.

" Forbear, forbear, my dear, I pity them, they know not what they are doing. They may shut me in where they please, but they cannot shut out God from me, and, for my part, I am as content to be here as in the Castle, and as content in the Castle as in the Tower of London, and as content there as when at liberty, and I hope to be as content on the scaffold as any of them all."

" Shortly you will envy me," he said, addressing his friends, " who am got before you. Mind that I tell you it, my skill fails if you will not ' *suffer much or sin much.*' " A sentiment he expressed also on the scaffold.

On the morning of his death he rose in usual spirits and transacted his business.

"What cheer, my Lord?" asked George Hutchison, a venerable minister of Edinburgh.

"Good cheer, sir," he answered; "the Lord hath said to me from heaven, Son! be of good cheer, thy sins are forgiven thee. God is good to me, that He lets not out too much of His communications here, for He knows I could not bear it."

After dinner with his friends, he retired for secret prayer.

In descending the stairs of the prison he called for James Guthrie, also under sentence of death for his adhesion to the Covenanting cause. They embraced each other.

"My Lord, God hath been with you. He is with you. He will be with you; and such is my respect for your Lordship, that, if I were not under sentence of death myself, I could cheerfully die for you."

On mounting the scaffold he saluted the people assembled. After prayer, by Mr Hutchison, the Marquis addressed the people.

"I come not here to justify myself but the Lord who is holy in all His ways. I desire not the Lord to judge any man, nor do I judge any but myself. I wish that as the Lord hath pardoned me, so may he pardon them for this. We are tied by Covenants to religion and reformation. These times are likely to be either very sinning or suffering times; and let them make their choice. There is a sad dilemma in this business, sin or suffer; and surely he that will choose the better part will choose to suffer."

After taking leave of his friends, he gave to each a token. To the executioner he gave a handkerchief and some money. He then knelt in secret prayer, and when ready he gave the signal, by raising his right hand. His body was taken to his home, and his head was stuck up at the Tolbooth.

Truth must be paid for, and the Marquis of Argyle was the first of those who laid down their lives for the sake of pure religion in the Covenanting struggle. He had faults many, as the best of men have, but that he was pure in his desire to see Truth reign in Scotland there can be no doubt. Like one of old, he preferred the sorrows of the children of God rather than the pleasures of royalty.

III.

REV. JAMES GUTHRIE.

THE other victim that Middleton had set his mind upon, was the fearless, godly preacher—James Guthrie of Stirling. By the death of two such men as Guthrie and Arygle it was intended to paralyse Scotland by fear.

Like so many of the ministers of those days Guthrie came from an ancient and noble family, his father being the Laird of Guthrie.

There is this, however, that marks Guthrie from most of his companions in the Covenanting struggle: he was born and brought up in the Episcopalian Church. Indeed, his father was such a strong defender of Episcopacy that it was his wish that James should belong to the ministry of that body.

Accordingly, he received the best education the grammar school could give, and then he went to St Andrews. Here he manifested such talent, that he became lecturer in philosophy.

In his St Andrews' days he was known as a young man of thoughtfulness, and gifted with a mind free entirely from bigotry. It was this that made him listen attentively to what the Covenanters had to say.

He was especially fortunate in making the friendship

of that noble, pure-hearted, and thorough Covenanter—
Samuel Rutherford. The gentle spirit and great piety of
Rutherford drew Guthrie to the weekly prayer meeting.
Here he began to understand what the Covenanting
movement aimed at. Here he saw the life of the men
who were being persecuted for their belief. The night's
experience deeply impressed him, and from henceforth
he laid their sorrows and their aims upon himself.

"If ye abide in the Episcopal Church ye may be a
star of the first magnitude in it," said a friend to him.

"Ye can never betray the faith of your father by
taking the side of those who threaten the King's
authority?" asked his father.

His choice, however, was made, and he became known
as a staunch sympathiser with the popular party.

Having passed his trial sermons he was appointed
minister to Lauder, and at once became a power in the
church which he had chosen.

It was, however, after his removal to Stirling that
Guthrie took that active part in the Reformation, then
going on in Scotland, which eventually led to his death.

He took the side of the protestors when the unhappy
division weakened the Covenanting party. Indeed, so
strongly did he feel that there was no hope as long as
men trusted in Charles, that he preached against the
Resolution. For this he was summoned to Perth to
answer before the King and the Committee of Estates
for his action.

The substance of Guthrie's defence was this : He
owned the authority of the King in civil affairs, but, as
far as the Church and its affairs were concerned he
would not acknowledge the King's authority. "Christ

being the Head of the Church it behoves us to see that to Him only we render obedience."

Even when they pressed him to defend some doctrines he had preached at Stirling, he declined to accede to their request on the same grounds.

He was imprisoned for a time, and then the King ordered his release, and he returned to Stirling.

He knew, however, the temper of the King and his advisers, and was certain he would not be allowed to remain long at rest. The Court party evidently intended to take matters with a high hand, and Guthrie accordingly set himself to checkmate them. His preaching from this period had a more earnest ring about it, the "joy of suffering for Christ" being one of his favourite themes.

The futile attempt of Middleton to raise an army for the King, by which it was intended to crush the Covenanting party, brought Guthrie under the hatred of Middleton.

In the Assembly the conduct of Middleton was severely criticised, and by no one more than Guthrie.

"Our duty to God and our country at this present juncture is to excommunicate this man, who, of all others, has stirred up strife in our midst. It is not for the Church to keep silence whilst her enemies are trying to destroy pure religion in our land," said Guthrie.

Many were in favour of milder measures, but, at last, by a narrow majority, Guthrie's motion was carried, and he was appointed to excommunicate Middleton at Stirling.

The Committee of Estates now intervened on behalf of Middleton, and desired Guthrie to delay the sentence until the whole matter had been further considered. He was a man who despised weakness of this kind. Although he carried into the pulpit the letter which practically forbade him pronouncing the sentence, he ignored it.

"The hour has come for us to strike a blow at evil, and I would be a traitor to my Lord and Master if I failed to strike when I have the opportunity." Thus he expressed his feelings at this time.

Guthrie soon saw to his sorrow that the men of compromise and defection were the rulers of the hour, and he set his pen to work on behalf of the strict Covenanters. It was no surprise to him that his former friends turned against him, and, at the Assembly of St Andrews in 1657, he was deposed.

An attempt was made to get one of the Assembly's men in the place of Mr Bennett, his colleague, but Guthrie resisted their effort, and agreed that a Mr Rule should work with him. For this he was mobbed and stoned by the friends of the Assembly.

If evidence is required that Guthrie and those who fought by his side were loyal subjects, it is shown by the fact that Guthrie went to London to defend the King's right against Cromwell. He, even in his prayers in the pulpit, asserted the King's title before the officers of Cromwell, much to their astonishment. He was not therefore a mere republican. He was a Royalist of the strongest kind so long as the King did not interfere with religion.

Yet, soon after the Restoration, he was marked by Middleton as a victim of his anger. He had never forgotten that sentence of excommunication. Whilst

Guthrie and others were drawing up a paper of supplication to the King, they were arrested, and he was sent to Stirling Castle. Here he lay until February 20, 1661, when he was tried.

JAMES GUTHRIE.

The charge of treason made against him was proceeded with under the following heads:

1. That he endorsed the Western Remonstrance.

2. That he published a book entitled *The Causes of the Lord's Wrath*.

3. That he subscribed the " Humble Petition."

4. That he called together the King's lieges.

5. That he declared the King was not his judge in theological matters.

6. That he used treasonable expressions in 1650.

The speech Guthrie made at this time is preserved in Wodrow's *History*, and is marked by dignity and clear reasoning. He upholds his right to discuss the evils of the age, and declares boldly the limits of the King's authority. The cause for which he was prepared to suffer he defends ardently. It was a speech that would have made a deep impression on an unprejudiced Parliament.

He was allowed until the 29th to prepare his defence.

The trial, however, was a long one, owing to his able defence. After he had acknowledged the facts brought against him, he showed that these could not constitute treason.

" I did never propose or intend to speak or act anything disloyal, seditious, or treasonable against His Majesty's person, authority, or government, God is my witness; and what I have spoken, written, or acted in any of these things wherewith I am charged hath been merely and singly from a principle of conscience, that, according to the light given me of God, I might do my duty as a minister of the gospel. But because the plea of conscience alone, although it may extenuate, cannot wholly excuse, I do assert that I have founded my speeches, writings, and actings, in these matters, on the Word of God, and on the Doctrine, Confession of Faith, upon the National Covenant of Scotland, and the Solemn League and Covenant betwixt the three kingdoms. If these foundations fall, I must fall with them; but if these sustain and stand in judgment, as I hope they will, I cannot acknowledge myself, neither I hope will his

Majesty's Commissioner and the honourable Court of
Parliament judge me guilty either of sedition or treason."

Day by day the trial went on, the judges finding it
difficult to bring in the verdict they had arranged
beforehand. His final words besought the judges to
come to a decision.

"I humbly beg that having brought so pregnant and
clear evidence from the Word of God, so much divine
reason and human laws, and so much of the common
practice of the Kirk and Kingdom, in my defence, and
being already cast out of my ministry, out of my dwell-
ing and maintenance, myself and my family put to live
on the charity of others, having now suffered eight months'
imprisonment, your Lordships would put no other burden
upon me. I shall conclude with the words of the
prophet Jeremiah, ' Behold I am in your hands, do to
me what seemeth good to you ': I know for certain
that the Lord hath commanded me to speak all these
things; and that if you put me to death you shall bring
innocent blood upon yourselves and upon the inhabi-
tants of this city.

"My Lords, my conscience I cannot submit; but this
old crazy body and mortal flesh I do submit to do with
it whatever you will, whether by death, or banishment,
or imprisonment, or anything else; only I beseech you
to ponder well what profit there is in my blood, it is
not the extinguishing of me, and many others, that will
extinguish the Covenant and work of Reformation since
the year 1638. My blood, bondage, or banishment will
contribute more for the propagation of these things than
my life or liberty could do, though I should live many
years."

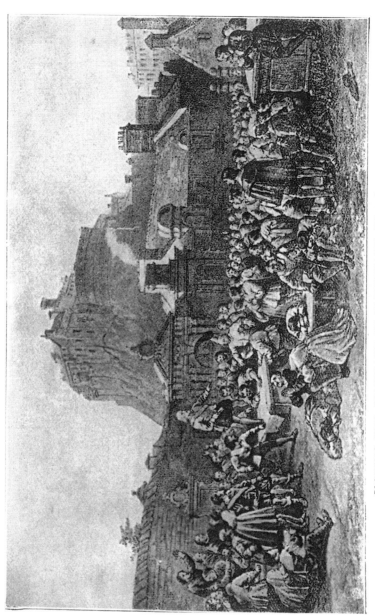

SIGNING THE COVENANT IN GREYFRIARS' CHURCHYARD.

The Marquis of Tweeddale voted for banishment, but nothing short of death would suit Middleton. Guthrie was, therefore, sentenced to be hanged at the cross of Edinburgh, but the day of his execution was not fixed.

When he received his sentence he turned to his judges and said :—" My Lords, let never this sentence affect you more than it does me, and let never my blood be required of the King's family."

Desperate efforts were made by several to save Guthrie. One class tried to tempt him to leave the Covenanters by the offer of a bishopric ; whilst others tried to get him to retract some of the things he had said. No doubt the intentions of these persons were good, but they deeply annoyed Guthrie. He, therefore, issued this declaration, which was duly witnessed :—

" These are to declare, that I do own the ' Causes of God's wrath,' the supplication at Edinburgh, August last, and the accession I had to the remonstrances. And if any do think, or have reported, that I was willing to recede from these, they have wronged me as never having any ground from me to think or to report so. This I attest under my hand at Edinburgh, about eleven o'clock, forenoon, before these witnesses."

June 1st was chosen as the day of Guthrie's death. During the interval he was cheerful in spirit, and very solicitous that his death should bear fruit to the glory of God.

On the evening before his execution, whilst sealing his letters, he stamped his letters crossways so as to obliterate his armorial bearings. When asked the cause of this he said :—

" I have no more to do with coat arms."

D

Whilst standing on the ladder, when about to be hung, he spoke for an hour with the composure of a man who was preaching in his pulpit, not his last words on earth.

"One thing I warn you all of, that God is very wroth with Scotland, and threatens to depart and remove his candlestick. The causes of this wrath are many, and would to God it were not one great cause, that the causes of wrath are disposed. Consider the case that is recorded in Jer. xxxvi., and the consequence of it, and tremble and fear.

"I do bear my witness to the National Covenant of Scotland and Solemn League and Covenant betwixt the three kingdoms. These sacred public oaths of God, I believe, can be loosed and dispensed with by no person, or party, or power upon earth, but are still binding upon these kingdoms, and will be so for ever hereafter, and are ratified and sealed by the conversion of many thousand souls since our entering thereunto. I take God to record upon my soul I would not exchange this scaffold with the palace or mitre of the greatest prelate in Britain. Blessed be God who hath showed mercy to me, such a wretch, and has revealed his Son to me, and made me a minister of the everlasting gospel, and that he hath deigned, in the midst of much tribulation from Satan and the world, to seal my ministry to the hearts of not a few of his people, and especially in the state wherein I was last, I mean the congregation of Stirling. Jesus Christ is my light and my life, my righteousness, my strength, and my salvation; yea, all my desire. Bless Him, O my soul, from henceforth even for ever."

The hangman here came to him and put the rope

round his neck, and covered his face with a napkin so that he might not see when he was to be turned off the ladder. The hangman was just preparing to perform his terrible work when Guthrie raised the napkin and cried with a loud voice of triumph :—

"The Covenants! The Covenants shall yet be Scotland's reviving!"

The death of Guthrie was a sore trial to the Covenanters. But his head, as it hung at the Nether Bow, had an effect on the Covenanters the Government did not expect. It moved the timid to be heroic, and robbed the cowardly of their weakness. In his death, more than his life, as he declared, he furthered the cause he so dearly loved.

IV

REV. HUGH M'KAIL

THE suppression of the Pentland rising was followed by a series of executions that made men sick of the sight of blood. The Prelates, ever ready to blacken the Covenanters, did all they could to make the prisoners taken at Rullion Green contemptible. After ten had been executed, their heads were set up at Hamilton, Kilmarnock, and Kirkcudbright, and their right hands at Lanark, where they had signed the Covenant. Another five were put to death a week later, and then a series of hanging spectacles were carried out all over the country, the poor men being hung at their own doors. Yet the men who were called upon to give up their lives were not cast down.

" We are assured, though this be the day of Jacob's trouble, that yet the Lord, when He hath accomplished the trial of His own, and filled up the cup of His adversaries, He will awake for judgment, plead His own cause, avenge the quarrel of His covenant, make inquiry for blood, vindicate His people, break the arm of the wicked, and establish the just—for to Him belongeth judgment and vengeance. And though our eyes shall not see it, yet we believe that the Sun of Righteousness shall arise with healing under His wings; and that He will revive His work, repair the breaches, build up the old wastes, and raise up the desolations; yea, the Lord will judge His people, and repent Himself for His servants, when their power is gone, and there is none shut up or left. We would not exchange lots with our adversaries, nor redeem our lives, liberties, and fortunes at the price of perjury and breach of the Covenant."

Mere hanging, however, became too common a sight, and torture was added to the death sentence. The instrument chosen was the terrible *boot*, which Gibbon describes:

> " 'Tis not enough felonious caves to fill,
> 'Tis not enough for cords and steel to kill,
> But on the ancle the sharp wedge descends,
> The bone reluctant with the iron bends ;
> Crushed is its frame, blood spouts from every pore,
> And the white marrow swims in purple gore."

The first victims of the *boot* were Neilson of Corsack and Hugh M'Kail. Both of these were connected with the Pentland rising, and both were put to death after horrible tortures.

Very little is known about the early days of Hugh M'Kail. He was born about 1640, and very early in life showed himself possessed of great parts.

> " His early dawnings sparkled such a light
> As promised a noon that should be bright,
> His greener blossoms gave such ample hope
> That none did question the succeeding crop.
> The Graces their own brother would have him styled,
> The Muses have adopted him their child ;
> Amongst her babes, him Eloquence has placed,
> And as her suckling, Pallas him embraced."

He was delicate in appearance, and considered very beautiful.

> " For he had beauty which might well endear,
>   No blemish in his body did appear ;
>   Some great thing sparkled in that blushing face,
>   Integrity that lovely brow did grace."

Hugh was the son of the minister of Bothwell, who had left his church rather than conform to the Prelates. He was thus brought up in an atmosphere which was impregnated with Covenanting hopes and ideas. This may account for the early stand he took in the Covenanting cause.

He was sent to Edinburgh to be educated, and stayed with his uncle, one of the ministers of that city. He showed himself possessed of a great mind, and advanced rapidly in his studies. A contemporary, from whom we have already quoted twice, describes him thus :

> " But whate'er were the beauties of his face,
>   A fairer mind dwelt in that lovely case ;
>   A sprightly mind, and unacquaint with guile,
>   Which with no baseness did itself defile ;
>   A divine soul, not made to vice a drudge,
>   A palace where the Graces chose to lodge."

The superior quality of M'Kail's mind and heart brought him in contact with some of the greatest men of his time. The Lord Provost of Edinburgh, Sir James Stewart, desiring a tutor for his family, was told about M'Kail. The Provost immediately made overtures which ended in Hugh becoming his chaplain and tutor to the family.

Sir James was a well-known supporter of the Covenanting cause, and at his table Hugh met such men as the

Earl of Argyle, the Earl of Loudon, Lord Warriston, and others.

It soon became apparent to all that days of trouble were close at hand, and Hugh was anxious to be ordained, that he might take his part in the struggle.

When only twenty-one years of age, therefore, he preached his trial sermons, and was licensed by the Presbytery of Edinburgh. His fame as a preacher soon spread over the city. Opportunities of preaching were given to him on every hand, and the more earnest hearts of the Covenanters declared M'Kail to be the "man for the hour."

His life as a preacher, however, was to be short. The 8th of September 1662 had been appointed as the last day on which non-conforming ministers were to retain their charges. Hugh had made up his mind to go out with his brethren rather than acknowledge the errors of Prelacy. His last sermon was preached in the High Church of Edinburgh, from Cant. i. 7. The burden of his message was the persecutions which the Church has had to suffer. His sentiments were thoroughly endorsed by his audience, and one sentence became at once historic.

"The Church has been persecuted by an Ahab on the Throne, a Haman in the State, and a Judas in the Church."

It did not take the country long to identify the men referred to. Middleton and Sharp knew that they had been rechristened; and under the plea "that Mr Hugh M'Kail, in a sermon preached in one of the kirks of Edinburgh, did most maliciously inveigh against and abuse His Most Sacred Majesty and the present Government in Church and State," macers were ordered to cite him before the Council against the 11th instant.

The company of horse that came to arrest Hugh could not find him, for he had escaped to his father's house, where he abode for some time. The search for him, however, was very keen; for the epithet "Judas" was now being hurled at Sharp from all quarters. M'Kail found it advisable, therefore, to leave the country, and went to Holland.

The three years spent in Holland were years of theological study. His eyes, however, were ever looking towards Scotland, and her troubles pressed heavily upon him. He was evidently maturing for the early death he felt was to be his.

On his return to Scotland things had not improved as he hoped, but had become much worse. Ignorant and profligate curates were in the manses of the land. Fines were imposed for non-attendance at the church. Men like Neilson had been fined and imprisoned for non-church-going. His wife and family had been driven from their home, and all his substance sold or wasted by the soldiers that were quartered upon them. Other and worse crimes were committed. Hugh was deeply stirred as he heard of these things from his father and others. One day in the week he spent in fasting and prayer for the poor persecuted people.

When, therefore, the people rose against the cruelties of Sir James Turner, and an appeal was made to the sword, Hugh at once made his way to the newly organised army.

The bad weather the Covenanters experienced as they marched through the country made many of them ill.

When at Ayr, Veitch mentions in his *Memoirs*, " Several
that were not used to such hardships were like to turn
valetudinary; and the worthy Hugh M'Kail would have
fallen off his horse if one had not laid hold of him and
kept him up; and they carried him into a house in that
fainting fit, laying him in a bed, and giving him something for a cordial by which his spirits returned, and he
recovered."

He was compelled to leave them near Cramond Water.
On his way to Liberton he was taken prisoner by an
officer of the dragoons.

Rothes believed the rising was a thoroughly organised
affair, but had failed as yet to get reliable information.
Perhaps this will in a measure modify our condemnation
of his cruelty. At any rate, he ordered the *boot* for
M'Kail. His youth and the delicate state of his health
had no effect upon the Council. Wedge after wedge was
driven home, as he could only confess the rising was the
natural rebound of Sir James Turner's cruelties.

" One touch more," cried the cruel Rothes, and the
bones cracked as the mallet fell.

" I protest solemnly, in the presence of God," cried
M'Kail; " I can say no more, though all the joints in my
body were in as great torture as that poor leg."

Seeing they could get nothing out of him further,
he was condemned to die with some others. When he
heard his sentence, he answered: " The Lord giveth and
the Lord taketh away, blessed be the name of the Lord."

When he arrived back at the prison he spent much
time in prayer. He then joined a friend in conversation.

" Oh, how good news, to be within four days' journey

of enjoying the sight of Jesus Christ! I am not so much troubled at death as I have been at preaching a sermon."

It seemed impossible that M'Kail would suffer death, the verdict being so contrary to the evidence. The Duchess of Hamilton interceded with Rothes, and the Marchioness of Douglas besieged Sharp, whilst Dr Matthew M'Kail personally interviewed Sharp. The answer was the same: "The business is in the Justiciaries' hands, and I can do nothing."

Now that it was apparent he was to die, he set himself to comfort those who were similarly placed. He was full of cheerfulness, which surprised many.

"The fear of my neck makes me forget how painful my leg is," he said to one.

It was when he parted with his father that he suffered most.

"Hugh," said the old man, with a flood of tears, "I called thee a good olive tree of fair fruits, and now a storm hath destroyed the tree, and his fruits and branches. I have sinned; thou poor sheep, what hast thou done?"

"Through coming short of the fifth commandment I have come short of the promise, that my days should be prolonged in the land of the living. God's controversy with thee is for over-valuing thy children, especially myself." It was an hour of bitterness, but full of tender feeling and loving affection.

About five o'clock on the morning of his execution he awoke, and said to John Wodrow:

"Up, John! You are too long in bed; you and I look not like men going this day to be hanged, seeing we lie abed so long." But his mind soon changed to serious thoughts.

" Now, Lord, we come to Thy throne, a place we have not been acquainted with. Earthly kings' thrones have advocates against poor men, but Thy throne hath Jesus, an advocate for us. Our supplication this day is not to be free of death, nor of pain in death, but that we may witness before many witnesses a good confession."

He was most anxious that all who were to die with him might not falter at the last, and much of the morning was spent in discussing how they were to behave before the people.

A thrill of emotion passed through the mob as Hugh came up to the platform. His crippled foot appealed to their imaginations, and we are told " there was such a lamentation as was never known in Scotland before ; not one dry cheek upon all the street or in all the numberless windows in the market-place."

For a little it nearly unnerved him.

" Your work is not to weep, but to pray that we may be honourably borne through—blessed be God that supports me ! "

He then read to them the last chapter of the book of Revelations. Passing the book to a friend, he began to speak to the people :

" Although I be judged and condemned as a rebel amongst men, yet I hope, even in order to this action, to be accepted as loyal before God. Nay, there can be no greater act of loyalty to the King, as the times now go, than for every man to do his utmost for the extirpation of that abominable plant of Prelacy, which is the bane of the throne and of the country. I heartily submit myself to death, as that which God hath appointed to all men because of sin."

The hangman then came to that part where the rope is put round the prisoner's neck. When this had been submitted to, he continued:

" I hope you perceive no alteration in my countenance; you may wonder at it, as I do, but I will explain it all. Besides the justness of my cause, this is my comfort, which was said of Lazarus when he died, that the angels did carry his soul into Abraham's bosom; it is to come into Christ's hands, and He will present it blameless and faultless to the Father, and then shall I be ever with the Lord."

He stood upon the ladder ready for the hangman to do his strange work. Lifting the handkerchief that covered his face, he added, with a heavenly glow upon his face:

" As there is a great solemnity here, a scaffold, a gallows, and people looking out of windows, so there is a greater and more solemn preparation in heaven of angels to carry my soul to God."

" Now I leave off to speak any more to creatures, and turn my speech to Thee, O Lord. Now I begin my intercourse with God, which shall never be broken off. Farewell, father and mother, friends and relations. Farewell, the world and all delights. Farewell, meat and drink. Farewell, sun, moon, and stars. Welcome, God and Father. Welcome, sweet Lord Jesus, the mediator of the New Covenant. Welcome, blessed Spirit of Grace, God of all consolation. Welcome, glory. Welcome, eternal life. Welcome, death."

At the early age of twenty-six Hugh M'Kail had won the martyr's crown. The vast crowd burst into sobbing as his fair form hung in the air. The Covenant was demanding the best blood of the land, and the men were ready to lay their life down for it. Men with keener insight would have seen that the cause that had at its service the best blood of the land *must* prevail. But these place-seekers, anxious to add to what they had, could see nothing but the plain fact, that their tyranny was being challenged, and that some men were bold enough to expose their wickedness.

V.

REV. DONALD CARGILL.

IN the end of June 1896, the Reformed Presbyterian Churches of the world, by their delegates, met at Rattray, Blairgowrie, to do honour to one of the great names in the Covenanting struggle—Donald Cargill. More than two thousand persons assembled near the spot where the house of the Covenanter stood, and where many Conventicles were held, and there paid eloquent tributes to one who whilst dead yet speaks.

The fact that there were four Donald Cargills living in the same district, at the same period, has caused some difficulty in finding when the martyr was born. The preponderance of evidence, however, seems to establish as fact that he was born at the "Ha' town" of Rattray about 1619.

His father was a small landowner, and this explains the liberal education Donald received; for, after attending a school at Rattray, he went to Aberdeen, and then to the University of St Andrews, where he distinguished himself as a student in philosophy.

His father, with the commendable ambition of a Scotsman, desired his cleverest and best son to devote his life to the work of the ministry. The son, however, had some hesitation in the matter. The ministry was a task much more difficult in those days than in the present time. Yet it had as much glory and honour then as now.

The words of his father, however, sank deep into his heart.

" And why should I not be one of the sacrifices ? " he asked himself. " Dare I choose mine own ease when the work of our Lord, perhaps, has need of my service ? "

He made the subject a matter of prayer, and the words of Ezekiel seemed to ring in his heart: " Son of man, eat this roll and go speak unto the house of Israel." From that hour he deemed himself " called " of God.

He soon received a license to preach, and began to take an active part in the movement which was then agitating the Kirk, to resist the innovations thrust upon her by the Royalists of the time.

In 1655 he was ordained minister of the Barony Church of Glasgow, a church that had in its midst a powerful faction opposed to the Covenanters. A church divided in this manner was no pleasure to a minister then, as it is no pleasure now. He accordingly determined to leave it, as he saw no hope of his preaching doing any good. He had gone so far as to mount, and was bidding some of his friends farewell, when a woman arrested him.

" Sir, you have promised to preach on Thursday, and have you appointed a meal for poor starving people, and will you go away and not give it ? If you do, the curse of God will certainly go with you."

He at once dismounted and settled down to his work as a minister, receiving much kindness from those who were of the Covenanting interest, and enduring much bitterness of soul through the Royalists.

It was the service commanded to be held to com-
memorate the Restoration that brought Cargill before
public notice. On entering the pulpit on the Sunday, a
large congregation awaited him. He believed they had
come there to rejoice at the Restoration, and his soul was
moved with indignation.

" We are not come here to keep this day upon the
account for which others keep it. We thought once to
have blessed the day wherein the King came home again,
but now we think we shall have reason to curse it ; and
if any of you come here to the solemnising of this day,
we desire you to depart. My text is, ' Rejoice not, O
Israel, for joy, as other people,' Hos. ix. 1.

" This is the first step of our going a-whoring from God ;
and whoever of the Lord's people this day are rejoicing,
their joy will be like the crackling of thorns under a pot,
it will soon be turned to mourning ; the King will be the
woefullest sight that ever the poor Church of Scotland saw :
woe, woe, woe unto him. His name shall stink while
the world stands, for treachery, tyranny, and trickery."

On the Monday morning a company of dragoons
were in search of Cargill. He was sitting in his study
when the thundering of the troopers was heard at the
door.

" You must hide, for your life is at stake," said the
lady with whom he lived.

" Leave it to me," he said, quietly ; and, slipping on a
lady's apron, he went to the door.

" Is that vile traitor, Donald Cargill here ? "

" Donald Cargill, the minister of Barony, is here, if
that is who you seek."

" In and lay hold of him," said the sergeant, and

Cargill rushed out, and found refuge in the house of one of his friends.

Cargill now took to preaching in the court-yards and narrow streets of Glasgow. Sentries were put at all the street corners to give him the signal when the soldiers came.

Standing on a chair he declared to the people the Word of God, and tried to stir them up to endurance of suffering rather than acquiesce in the demands of the Government. He was a man who believed in small congregations. Not more than half-a-dozen would stand around him, but the people looked from out their windows or stood at their doors. They dare not manifest their sympathy with him, save when the cry " Dragoons " was heard. The fact that he escaped so often was due to the kindliness of heart of the people who listened to him.

The failure of Middleton to lay hold of Cargill caused the Government to pass an Act whereby Cargill was not allowed to come south of the Tay. He disregarded this, however, and became a field preacher, equalling John Knox in his earnest outspokenness against the vices of high and low, not excepting the clergy themselves, many of whom he denounced for accepting the seductive " Indulgence."

The more soldiers they sent after Cargill the more friends helped him to defeat the plans of the dragoons. The country was rising fearlessly against the Government, and, at last, in a friendly way, they cited him to appear before them. He obeyed their summons and appeared before them on November 23, 1668. Here he boldly avowed the truths that the Council were trying to suppress. They became indignant, and it seemed as though they would have condemned him to death, but his friends in the Council got him released after being cautioned.

Their timidity increased his boldness. His street preaching began at once; and, in anger, they began to seek him. Through his friends in the Council he agreed not to reside in Glasgow or Edinburgh if the Council withdrew his banishment to the north of the Tay. This they agreed to, without exactly knowing what it all meant.

He was at the Conventicle which ended as the battle of Bothwell Bridge. He was not a preacher only but a fighter, and was severely wounded in the head. After the rout a dragoon made him prisoner, but, on finding he was a minister, Cargill was at once released.

He was now looked upon as one of the chief leaders in the Covenanting struggle. And as the author of the " Queensferry Paper " he became the terror of the Government. They were sure that Cargill was at the root of a huge plot to massacre the King and his leading advisers. Yet this famous paper was simply the jottings of a conversation. It came into the Government's hands in the following manner :

While Cargill and Henry Hall of Haughhead were hiding in the neighbourhood of Queensferry, information of their whereabouts was given to the Governor of Blackness Castle, by the Curate of Borrowstounness. A small company of soldiers came to arrest them, and they at once resisted. Cargill was overpowered, but Hall rushed at the captor, and Cargill got free. Hall, however, was taken prisoner, and died on the road to Edinburgh. In his pocket was found a paper, notes of

Cargill's talk. This was the famous " Queensferry Paper."
Some of the things it contained were very startling.

" We do reject the King and those associate with him
in the Government from being our King and rulers."

Cargill made no apology for this position. The
necessity of the age required it, and following events
showed his wisdom.

In conjunction with Cameron he issued the " Sanquhar
Declaration," which formally and publicly threw off allegiance to the King, since to obey the King was to dis-
honour God.

The Government retaliated by offering a large reward
for the arrest of Cargill. He was now at the mercy of
every covetous wretch in the country. Scarcely a meeting was held but disquieting alarms were given : for the
dragoons seemed everywhere. He had a narrow escape
when he held service in a field some miles out of Glasgow. He had been assured that all was safe, and had
begun his sermon when he noticed a heavy dust on the
road. He at once disbanded the meeting, and they
scattered in all directions. It was discovered that one,
who pretended to be a most ardent supporter of the
Covenanting cause, had gone for the dragoons, as soon as
he knew Cargill had determined to preach.

It had long lain upon the heart of Cargill that it was
time for the Church to be the aggressor. He, therefore,
at Torwoodlee, near Stirling, carried his thoughts into
practice by excommunicating the King and his chief
supporters. His words filled many of his hearers with
dismay, but they were words of reason to Cargill. After
he had preached his sermon he raised his hands to heaven
in prayer. The woes of his country were the burden of

this prayer. He besought God's wisdom in the hour of distress, and concluded with a tender appeal to the Almighty to comfort the poor hunted Covenanters. Then came the solemn excommunication :

" I, being a minister of Jesus Christ, and having authority and power from Him, do, in His name, and by His spirit excommunicate, cast out of the true Church, and deliver to Satan, Charles the Second, King of Great Britain and Ireland, the Duke of York, the Duke of Monmouth, the Duke of Lauderdale, the Duke of Rothes, General Dalziel, and Sir George Mackenzie."

The Presbyterian party, as a whole, repudiated this act of Cargill's, but their repudiation was not to their honour, for it was done as a matter of expediency. They endorsed the sentiment of Cargill's excommunication.

This bold stroke filled the minds of all concerned with great consternation, for excommunication meant not only the loss of spiritual privileges, but it robbed the excommunicated of his social and political rights. And it was only after the Presbyterian party repudiated Cargill's action that the Government calmed down a bit.

Yet their feeling is expressed in the fact that they raised the reward for Cargill's apprehension to 5000 merks. Lord Rothes, in fact, never got over the curse of Cargill.

" We all thought little of what that man Cargill did in excommunicating us," said Lord Rothes, on his death-bed, " but I find that sentence binding upon me *now*, and it will bind to Eternity."

Cargill had many narrow escapes after this. Middleton was very anxious to lay hands on him, and for this purpose used a professing Covenanter named Henderson, whose avarice made him willing to betray Cargill.

He forged letters in the name of some saintly men in Fife, and went to Edinburgh and put these letters into the hand of Cargill. They contained an earnest appeal to Cargill to come and preach at Beith.

"I will go to them," said Cargill, and Henderson was elated.

"Let me see your clothes that I may know you well," he said, "for foes are plentiful." After he had made the inspection, he added, "I will have a boat ready to take you over the Forth." And he hurriedly left them and went straight to Middleton's soldiers, and ordered them to get out of sight as Cargill was coming.

It so happened that several friends of Cargill started to walk to the Forth in advance, and Cargill and Mr Boig were to follow on horseback. This was one particular Henderson had not learned, and the lack of it defeated his avaricious plans.

"Here they are, now let us out and lay hands on them all," said the sergeant. The soldiers burst out upon the travellers, and in their eagerness to secure Cargill, they took little heed of the ladies. One of them ran back to Edinburgh and informed Cargill of what had taken place, and he thus escaped, much to the chagrin of Henderson and the soldiers.

Cargill now saw it was impossible to trust himself to any man, and for a time he retired to England. But his heart was in Scotland and he came to Lanark.

He arranged to preach at Loudonhill, and soon a large number of people collected there, and outposts were put along the roads. He was not disturbed, however, and after preaching, he baptised eight children. Other mothers hearing of the service brought their children, and another baptismal service was gone through. The people then pressed him to preach again, and he agreed to do so.

The 5000 merks reward was too much, however, for some who were at the first preaching, and they hurried off to Glasgow to inform the soldiers where Cargill was. With great haste they rode out of Glasgow, sure of their prey. Cargill was about to pronounce the Benediction when a boy informed him that the soldiers were coming.

" Fear not little flock ; it is your Father's good pleasure to give you the Kingdom," he said to the people. " Save yourselves from these blood-thirsty men, and let each aid the other."

Wildly the women and children ran hither and thither seeking a shelter. Some of the men were for resisting, but Cargill cried " Not now, not now." He himself took a road that, instead of being a refuge, was bringing him straight into the road where the soldiers were. One of his friends hailed him to the Moss, and though the soldiers fired at the fugitives, no one was hurt, and all escaped.

He felt that his days were to be few, for the enemy was for ever close upon his heels. He had gone through Ayrshire and Galloway, preaching in the valleys or on the hilltops. Many of his meetings were disturbed, but he always escaped.

He had gone to Dunsyre Common, between Clydesdale and Lothians, to preach, and chose as his text, Isaiah xxvi. 20, " Come, my people, and enter thou into thy chambers."

A TYPICAL BIT OF COVENANTING COUNTRY.

News of this meeting reached the ears of James Irvine of Bonshaw, and the thought of 5000 merks made him determine to capture Cargill. He allowed the meeting to take place, and then set a watch on Cargill. Early in the morning, with a company of dragoons, he came to Covington Mills, where Cargill was staying. On laying his hands upon Cargill, he exclaimed :

" O blessed Bonshaw, and blessed day that ever I was born, that has found such a prize—a prize of 5000 merks for apprehending of him this morning."

Cargill was hurried off to Lanark jail, and there they rested for a little. He was then taken out and put on a bare-backed horse, Bonshaw himself tying Cargill's feet below the horse's belly. This gave the prisoner great pain.

" Why do you tie me so hard ? Your wickedness is great," said Cargill. " You will not long escape the just judgment of God ; and, if I be not mistaken, it will seize you in this very place."

His final destination was Edinburgh, where he was brought before the Council. It shows how keenly they felt the excommunication at Torwoodlee, for this was the chief theme of their questioning. He, however, declined to discuss the matter with them, as it was a religious, not a civil, excommunication. They pressed him on other matters, the answers he gave being, in the eyes of the Council, rank rebellion.

Some of the Council, as they looked at the old grey-haired man, stricken in years, were moved to ask that he be sent to the Bass for life.

" To the gallows," said Lord Rothes, bitterly, and so it was decided.

" Your death shall be one of extreme torture," hissed Lord Rothes.

" My Lord Rothes, forbear to threaten me, for die what death I will, your eyes shall not see it "—a prophecy that came true, for Lord Rothes took suddenly ill, and died before Cargill was hanged.

Being brought to the scaffold, he opened his Bible, and turning to Psalm cxviii, he commenced from verse 16, and sang sixteen lines :

> " The right hand of the mighty Lord
>   Exalted is on high ;
> The right hand of the mighty Lord
>   Doth ever valiantly.
>
> I shall not die, but live, and shall
>   The works of God discover ;
> The Lord hath me chastened sore,
>   But not to death given o'er.
>
> O set ye open unto me
>   The gates of righteousness ;
> Then will I enter into them,
>   And I the Lord will bless.
>
> This is the gate of God, by it
>   The just shall enter in ;
> Thee will I praise, for thou me heard'st,
>   And hast my safety been."

He then began to address the people, but an order was given for the drums to beat.

" Ye see we have no liberty to speak what we would, but God knoweth our hearts," he cried. This shot evidently hit the sergeant, for the drums ceased and Cargill was allowed to speak.

" Now I am as sure of my interest in it, and peace with

God, as all within this Bible and the Spirit of God can make me; and I am fully persuaded that this is the very way for which I suffer, and that He will return gloriously to Scotland, but it will be a terror to many; therefore, I beseech you, be not discouraged at the way of it, and the cause for which I am to lay down my life and step into Eternity, where my soul shall be as full of Him as it can deserve to be; and now, this is the sweetest and most

DONALD CARGILL'S BIBLE

glorious day that ever mine eyes did see. Now I am near the getting of the crown which shall be sure, for which I bless the Lord, and desire all of you to bless Him, that he hath brought me here and made me triumph over devils, men, and sin."

Then having prayed privately, he raised the napkin from his face and said :

"Farewell, all relations and friends in Christ; farewell, acquaintances and earthly enjoyments; farewell, reading and preaching, praying and believing, wanderings, reproach, and sufferings. Welcome, Father, Son, and Holy Spirit; into Thy hands I commit my spirit." And the hangman turned him off the ladder, and Cargill was dead.

The Bible that Cargill used on the scaffold was used at the service referred to at the beginning of this chapter, and, by the courtesy of a descendant of the noble Cargill, we give a reproduction of it on the previous page.

VI.

THE WIGTON MARTYRS.

THE story of the Wigton martyrs reveals so much of fiendish cruelty, that every effort has been made to throw discredit upon the story. The more it has been investigated, however, the more apparent is the fiendish cruelty. The most ardent supporter of the Covenanters to-day would be intensely glad if it could be proved that the Wigton martyrs were not historical. The shameful picture of human degradation presented is an everlasting disgrace to humanity.

The chief figure of the martyrdom was Margaret Wilson, a young woman of eighteen years of age, famed for her nobleness of life, kindness of heart, and sympathetic generosity to all in distress.

Very early in life she became a follower of the Lord Jesus Christ, and by her influence her brother and sister also became Christians.

Her father and mother attended the Episcopal Church, as by law they were compelled to do, under the death penalty, but the three children attended the field meetings held by the Covenanters.

Their youth protected them for a time from the fury of the oppressors, and their absence from the parish church was winked at. Whether it was because Mr Wilson had a little property, or because there were few people to persecute, we cannot say, but one morning Margaret Wilson, aged eighteen, Thomas, aged sixteen, and Agnes, aged thirteen were reported by the curate as defaulters in church attendance.

" Send the dragoons after them," said the cruel Grierson of Lagg, " and we'll teach them their duty."

A friendly hint was given to the Wilsons that the children were to be arrested, and a family council was held. It will surprise us to find the intelligent grasp the children had, not only of the Bible, but of the aims and objects of the Covenanters.

" We judge you not, mother, but were we to attend the curate's church, it would be sinning against our Lord. He neither teaches the Word of God, nor does he endeavour to live it, as his drunken habits declare. To sit in his church means acknowledging all the King has done, which we cannot do. It sanctions the persecution of the poor Covenanters, whose only fault is they will worship God in as pure a manner as they possibly can. Our hearts are with these hunted men, and we will share willingly in their sufferings."

And that night, after an affectionate farewell, the three wandered out to the moss-hags in search of a hiding-place from the dragoons.

When the soldiers arrived at Wilson's house, they were greatly surprised to find the children were not at home.

" Then, if you ever allow them to enter your house, or if you ever send them food, we will take you outside your own door and shoot you," said the sergeant to the mother. " Tell me where they are hiding."

" We know not where they are. They left here last

night, preferring to endure suffering sooner than agree
to the demand they felt certain you would make upon
them."

" We'll make greater demands than ever when we find
them. Let's be after them, men."

The dragoons searched all the caves they knew, and
pierced every thick bush with their sword, and travelled
over the moss, but the Wilsons were safe. About a
hundred soldiers in all were quartered at Mr Wilson's
house, at great expense to him. He bore it patiently,
even when they fined him. In all he lost 5000 merks.

The cave in which these noble children hid may be seen
to-day by the curious. It has slightly altered its form
through frosts and rain. It has been formed by two
large slabs of stone, like the legs of an A, resting against
each other. A small stone covers the mouth of it, and
this was covered by some wild brambles and tufts of
heather. It was small, wet, and necessarily uncomfort-
able, but here they spent the whole day, and at night
searched for food.

On the death of Charles II., when the country was
filled with hopes of a more lenient policy, the young
Wilsons were advised by some of their Covenanting
friends that they could now go safely home. They were
a little timid about going to their parents' house, and
went rather to the house of a widow, about seventy
years of age, named Margaret M'Lauchlan. This woman
was the other victim that sealed her testimony with her
life.

Whilst at the widow's house, Margaret Wilson met a
man named Patrick Stuart, whom she knew well, and
who had received much kindness from her father. She

inquired about her parents and others, and he gladly
gave her all the news he knew. He was exceedingly
attentive to her, and when he heard the story of their
sufferings in the cave, he invited them to come next
evening and partake of refreshments at his house. This
they consented to do, trusting him, as to offer hospitality
to Covenanters was a crime heavily punished.

There is a tradition to the effect that Patrick had been
a suitor for the hand of Margaret, but that she gave him
little encouragement. When they came to his home
next evening, he renewed his offer of marriage, which
she declined. He then asked her to drink to the King's
health, which she promptly refused to do. Without a
word of warning or farewell he left the room, went
straight to the Wigton authorities, and informed them
where the Wilson children were.

Soon a company of dragoons sought them out, and the
two girls were arrested and thrown into the horrible
place called "The Thieves' Hole."

When Patrick informed on the Wilsons, partly through
spite, and partly for the reward he received, he also informed upon the aged Margaret M'Lauchlan, for entertaining the Wilsons. She was arrested soon after the
two Wilsons, and thrust into prison.

Their sufferings in prison are part of the horribleness
of their persecution. They were only supplied with food
once a day, and that was of poor quality and quantity.
They had no beds to lie upon, and lay down on the damp
cell at nights. No complaint ever came from their lips,
however, for they accepted all that came to them as part
of the price they had to pay for their witnessing for God.

Now that they had been taken prisoners, it was found

rather difficult to get a reasonable charge against them. It required little in those days, however, to be sentenced to death.

They were brought before the infamous Sir Robert Grierson, of Lagg, and charged with being at the battle of Bothwell Bridge, Ayr's Moss, at twenty field conventicles, and a like number of house conventicles.

" We were never near Bothwell Bridge in our life," said Margaret Wilson, " and even if we had, we were only twelve and seven years of age when that took place. We were never at Ayr's Moss either."

" Then you were at conventicles," thundered Grierson.

" Yea, we have, and prefer them much to the dead preaching of the curates, whose hearts are blind. But there is nothing worthy of death in worshipping God in a pure manner on the hillside."

" Give them the abjuration oath," shouted Grierson to an officer in Court.

By this oath the Covenanters were made to abjure a manifesto issued by the Cameronians, in which they renounced the authority of Charles Stuart, condemned the killing of those who differed in judgment, and in which they declared they would stand up for their rights as religious men and women.

All the three women refused to take this oath, as the Court expected.

" To death then, to death," shouted that monster of iniquity, Grierson, and he then passed sentence.

" Upon the 11th of May ye shall be tied to stakes fixed within the flood-mark in the water of Blednock, near Wigton, where the sea flows at high water, there to be drowned."

In the wildest moments of fear they had never expected such an inhuman sentence. The whole of Wigton was filled with excitement, and Mr Wilson at once hurried to Edinburgh to intercede with the Privy Council on behalf of his daughters. He managed to get the youngest daughter liberated on paying a fine of 100 merks, the last of the poor man's money.

Margaret Wilson was besieged in prison by her friends, who used all their powers to get her to take the abjuration oath. The terrible grief of her mother tried her sore, especially when the mother upbraided her for lack of obedience to her parents.

" If my father and my mother forsake me, the Lord will take me up," she said, with tears in her eyes.

" I did not mean that," said the mother hysterically, " but the sword hath pierced my soul. Could you not relent so far as to promise to listen to the curate, Sunday by Sunday."

" That were to acknowledge Prelacy as right, and deny that the hill folk are right." She was unmovable.

The widow made an appeal to the Privy Council, in which she offered to take the oath of abjuration. She appealed to her age as another reason why she should be left alone.

The Secretaries of State granted a reprieve to the two women, as the Register of the Acts of the Privy Council attest, but the reprieve was never put into force. Why this was so has never been satisfactorily explained—save it be that Lagg had no wish to be cheated out of the sport it would be to him to see two women put to death in this novel and barbarous manner.

On the 11th of May, Major Windram with a troop of

From a Painting by G. Harvey.

THE BATTLE AT AYR'S MOSS.

soldiers came to the Tolbooth of Wigton and demanded the two prisoners.

It was a beautiful May morning, and the crowds of people dressed in their best attire made it look more like a gala than a procession of death.

The sight of the two large stakes erected in the sand, one thirty yards further out than the other, took the colour from the cheeks of more than the prisoners. Women began to weep, and men began to clench their fists and grind their teeth. It required but one man to lead, and they would have torn the soldiers to pieces; but the leader was not there.

"We are called upon this day to give a worthy testimony for our Lord. He hath done us much good and no ill these years we have served Him. This day shall we behold Him in the glory of His risen power, and I do rejoice the end is so near at hand," said Margaret to the widow, who had now become courageous.

The widow was marched out to the stake nearest the sea and there tied securely. It was hoped to break the spirit of the young woman by the sight of the widow's death. Possibly they were afraid that unless the widow was drowned speedily she would recant, and so spoil their fiendish sport.

Slowly the sea in golden crests crept along the sand and lapped the widow's feet, as though hungering to devour her.

"Though I walk through the valley of the shadow of death I will fear no evil, Thy rod and Thy staff they comfort me," she said, quietly, and her face had a new light in it, as though the sea, gilded with the golden sun, had reminded her of the City of God.

F

Higher and higher came the water, and the women on the beach turned their heads away as it reached her waist, and at the same time touched the feet of Margaret Wilson.

"The Lord will this day cleave the waters of death asunder for me, and I shall behold the Lamb in his beauty," she cried out to the weeping mob.

The water had now reached the widow's neck, and Lagg and others began to make sport of her as they saw her strain her neck to keep out of the water. A wave passed over her, and the struggle of death began. Margaret Wilson saw the struggles of the widow, and her voice was raised in prayer that God would take Margaret M'Lauchlan to Himself.

"What thinkest thou of that?" said a soldier to Wilson, pointing to the death-struggles of the widow.

"What do I think! I see Christ in one of His members wrestling there. Think you that we are the sufferers? No, it is Christ in us, for He sends none a warfare upon their own charges."

She then began to sing the 25th Psalm, and those on the beach who had lost their timidity joined her in some of the lines:

> "The Lord is good and gracious,
>   He upright is also;
> He therefore sinners will instruct
>   In ways that they should go."

The sharp turning of the soldiers smartly silenced them, however.

As the water crept on towards her shoulders, she closed her eyes in prayer. Her mother rushed to the edge of the water, and besought her with tears to say, "God save the King."

THE BEGINNING OF THE END. MARGARET WILSON TIED TO THE STAKE

" Pray with me mother that I may not fail at the last moment," was her reply. And her eyes closed again, and her lips moved.

A great hush came over the crowd, which was only broken by the jeers of Grierson.

" God receive my spirit," said Margaret, as the water once or twice lapped her face. There was the gasping of drowning, and, to the joy of all, a soldier rushed into the water, cut Margaret's bonds, and brought her to the shore.

The people shouted with glee, and the mother wept for joy. It was unheard of mercy, and though Margaret seemed more dead than alive, the remedies they used soon restored her to consciousness.

It was then seen that the mercy was the work of a fiend, and not of a human heart. Lagg's sport was too soon coming to an end, and he had restored her to life to torture her again. Major Windram went forward and began to test her.

" Will you pray for the King ? "

" I wish the salvation of all men and the damnation of none," she answered meekly.

" Oh, Margaret, why will you throw away your life," said her mother in terrible agony. " Say ' God save the King, God save the King.' "

" God save him if He will; for it is what I often have prayed for, and do pray for now. But, mother, you do not understand these monsters."

" Sir, my daughter hath said it, she hath said it, let her go free," said the mother, frantically, throwing herself at the Major's feet.

Margaret had meanwhile closed her eyes in prayer.

She knew, instinctively, that they had determined on her death.

" See, my daughter is praying for the King," said Mrs Wilson, pointing to her daughter.

" We want none of her prayers," said the brutal Lagg. " Tender her the abjuration oath, and, if she refuse, let her drink some more of the sea."

" I am ready for death ; I will not take the oath. I trust God may forgive you this murder before your hour of death comes. I am one of Christ's children, and have done naught worthy of death."

" Back to the sea, back to the sea with the hag," cried Lagg, and two soldiers lifted her in their arms, waded in as far as they could, and then flung her headlong into the sea. They then pushed her head under the water with the butt end of their guns.

In this fiendishly-cruel manner died two innocent, noble women. This crime has caused several names to stink in the nostrils of the world. Grierson of Lagg will ever be looked upon as a monster more that a man.

The story of the Wigton martyrs spread like fire over the length and breadth of Scotland, and inspired the Covenanters with joy that two of their number had been so faithful. It caused many Royalists to become friends of the Covenanters, afterwards. Three of the children of Major Windram from that hour were Covenanters in heart, and died as such.

If there was a sharpening of weapons amongst the Covenanters after this, who can blame them ? To defend oneself from such barbarity surely needs no excuse.

Two stones have been erected over the graves of these

two women, whose bodies lie in Wigton churchyard.
The memorial in Stirling churchyard will be familiar
to many of our readers. A transcription of the Wigton
stones may be of interest:

> " Here lies Margaret M'Lauchlan
> Who was by unjust law sentenced
> To die by Lagg, Strachan, Windram,
> And Grahame, and tied to a stake for her
> Adherence to Scotland's Reformation,
> Covenants, National, and Solemn League."

The other one reads as follows:

> " Let earth and stone still witness bear
> There lies a virgin-martyr here,
> Murdered for owning Christ supreme
> Head of His Church, and no more crime
> But not abjuring Presbytery,
> And her not owning Prelacy.
> They her condemned by unjust law ;
> Of heaven nor hell they stood in awe.
> Within the sea, tied to a stake,
> She suffered for Christ Jesus' sake.
> The actors of this cruel crime
> Were Lagg, Strachan, Windram, and Grahame.
> Neither young years nor yet old age
> Could stop the fury of their rage."

VIL

RICHARD CAMERON.

IT is the pride of some in Scotland to-day to call themselves " Cameronians." It is a title no man need be ashamed of, for it means " thoroughness," as well as " unselfish devotion to the Lord Jesus Christ." The name, as may be suspected, is derived from the leader of what was a new development in the Covenanting struggle.

About the early years of Richard Cameron we have little information. He was a Fifeshire man, being born at Falkland in that shire. His father was a small merchant, and seems to have given Richard a good education. He became schoolmaster in Falkland, and regularly attended the Episcopal Church.

It may have been gradual, but the final step was sudden. He resigned his position as schoolmaster, wiped the dust off his feet as regards Episcopacy, and became a Covenanter in deed and in truth.

Instantly he became an object of persecution, and determined to leave the joys of home and seek work elsewhere. He became tutor in the family of Sir William Scott of Harden. This position he did not hold long, however. The peculiar sincerity of Cameron, his contempt for compromises, made him refuse to attend the church his master went to. It was Presbyterian, but the minister had accepted the Indulgence, and so acknowledged the King's authority in religious matters. With mutual expressions of regret they parted, and Cameron joined himself to the saintly John Welch, who was holding conventicles in Teviotdale.

He was prevailed upon by Welch to preach, and did so. He was then asked to become a regular preacher, and after a time consented, and was ordained in the house of Harry Hall of Haughhead.

" If you this day ordain me to the ministry, you must not blame me if I declare all that God puts into my heart. If you ask me to preach on national sin, there is only one that is worth fighting, that is, the iniquity of accepting the Indulgence."

He began to preach through Annandale with much acceptance. Hardly a sermon was delivered without a scathing denunciation of those ministers, who, to save their flesh, had taken the Indulgence. This so aroused some of them, that Richard was requested to come to Edinburgh to be reprimanded. He went, and they deeply impressed him with the warning that he was making divisions in their midst.

" Unity is our need just now. There are more essential things to preach about than the Indulgence. Let that matter rest for the present."

To this Richard consented with some hesitation, and returned to his preaching.

The position Cameron had taken amongst the ousted ministers is seen by the fact that he preached before thousands at Maybole, where the Communion was to be dispensed.

A tent had been erected on the face of a small hill for the preacher. The crowd sat all about the preacher on the heather and grass. In front of Richard, on two small tables covered by spotless linen, were the Elements. Several ministers and elders stood by the side of the tables, as though guarding them. Under such impressive conditions, Cameron preached about the great sacrifice Christ offered when he died on the Cross. After the sermon, the Elements were dispensed to those who came forward.

His promise of silence on the question of the Indulgence filled Cameron with uneasiness. He felt he had no business, just for the sake of a temporary peace, to refrain from denouncing what his heart so bitterly condemned. He therefore went over to Holland to consult with several who had fled there. He preached in the Scots Kirk at Rotterdam, and rejoiced the hearts of all who heard him. The brethren there listened to his story, and advised him to declare all that was in his heart.

" Richard, the public standard has now fallen in Scotland," said Mr M'Ward, " and, if I know anything of the mind of the Lord, you are called upon to undergo your trials before us; go home, and lift the fallen standard, and display it publicly before the world; but before you put your hand to it, ye shall go to as many of the field ministers as ye can find, and give them your hearty invitation to go with you, and if they will not go along with you, go alone, and the Lord be with you."

At the next meeting, Mr M'Ward, Mr Brown, and Mr Roleman, a famous Dutch divine, laid their hands upon Cameron's head, and blessed him.

" Behold, all ye beholders," said Mr M·Ward, " here is the head of a faithful servant of Jesus Christ, who shall lose the same for his Master's interest, and it shall be set up before sun and moon in the view of the world."

With such an endorsement, Cameron returned to Scotland, and immediately took up a strong position. The people crowded to hear him wherever he went, and he took this as evidence that God was with him.

The defeat at Bothwell Bridge had made the ministers timid, and the people downhearted. The Government had issued more stringent laws against field meetings. The cause seemed hopeless. The voice of Cameron rang through Scotland like the blast of a trumpet. They looked for a leader, and God sent them Cameron.

It was the position Cameron took up in regard to the King that made him leader.

" The most part of the land cry out, ' We will have no other King but Cæsar, no other King but King Charles.' We must cry, ' We will have no other King but Christ.' What, say ye, are ye against monarchical government? We are not much taken up with that, if God let pure government be established, what is most for the advantage of civil and ecclesiastical society. If ever ye see good days in Scotland, without disowning the present King, believe me no more. Let them take heed unto themselves ; for though they should take us to scaffolds, and kill us in the fields, the Lord will yet raise up a party who will be avenged upon them. We had rather die than live in the same country with them, and outlive the glory of God departing altogether from these lands."

Donald Cargill and Douglas met and discussed with

Cameron the position he had taken up. They agreed to
issue a Declaration in which these ideas should be fully
expressed.

It was on June 22nd, 1680, the old town of Sanquhar
was startled by the noise of twenty horses riding into the
town. They rode straight to the old cross at the market-
place. Two men dismounted from their horses. These
were Richard and Michael Cameron. Michael then
engaged in prayer, the company sang a Psalm, and he
read the famous "Sanquhar Declaration," which begins
as follows: " We do, by these presents, disown Charles
Stuart, that has been reigning, or rather tyrannising, on
the throne of Britain these years bygone, as having any
right, title to, or interest in the Crown of Scotland for
Government, as forfeited several years since by his perjury
and breach of covenant, both to God and His Kirk, and
by his tyranny and breach of the very essential conditions of government in matters civil."

After it was all read, one engaged in prayer, and then
the twenty men rode out to the moors.

This was the most wicked treason then: it became a
lawful position to take up in 1688. Such are the changes
time makes.

A reward of 5000 merks was offered for the arrest of
Cameron, and he had to use every precaution for his
safety. He went about preaching all over the countryside, followed by twenty-three men on horseback and
forty on foot, all armed. News came to Cameron that
a large company of soldiers were searching for him. He
therefore made for Ayr's Moss, a large, dismal wilderness, stretching for miles between Cumnock and Muirkirk. Whether they had neglected to put outposts is

RICHARD CAMERON'S PRAYER BEFORE THE BATTLE OF AYR'S MOSS,
"Lord, spare the green and take the ripe."

not known; but the soldiers came suddenly upon Cameron, and he knew a fight was inevitable.

Cameron at once mounted his white horse, and the others assembled around him. His devotions were short, and one phrase only has come to us. Thrice he prayed: *" Lord, spare the green and take the ripe."* Then turning to his brother Michael, he said:

" Now let us fight it out to the last, for this is the day I have longed for, and the day I have prayed for, to die fighting against our Lord's avowed enemies."

They put themselves into the best position they could, and formed on a small hill, which was nearly surrounded by bogs. Cameron commanded eight horsemen, Hackston took the rest.

On came the dragoons as fast as they could, and down swept the Covenanters upon them. Cameron and his eight horsemen cut clean through the dragoons. There was no keeping them together, however, and soon it was every man fighting the best way he could. The Covenanters were only half the number of the dragoons. More than a dozen men rushed at Cameron, anxious to win the reward for his arrest. He slashed out right and left, and was pulled from his horse wounded all over. He was dead.

Robert Murray cut off his head and hands, and took them to the Council in Edinburgh, saying, as he laid them on the table:

" There are the head and hands of a man who lived praying and preaching, and died praying and fighting."

VIII.

FAITHFUL UNTO DEATH.

THE peasants of Scotland are marked by a deep religious life. If they are not educated in the higher forms of learning, they know their Bible well, and zealously try to obey God. Poor in this world's goods, they are rich toward God.

This could honestly be said of Isabel Alison, a native of Perth, aged 27, and Marion Harvey, a servant girl in Borrowstounness, aged 20, who found themselves in prison in Edinburgh because they were Covenanters.

Marion, when about 15 years of age, left the Episcopal Church and began to attend the hill meetings. She did this for some years unmolested, but a miserable wretch named Henderson, for the sake of the reward, informed the authorities, and she was stopped on her way to a field meeting.

" Are you going to a field meeting ? " inquired the sergeant of dragoons.

" I refuse to tell you where I am going," she said firmly.

" But your Bible there tells me that what Henderson said is true." And she was taken to Edinburgh.

Isabel Alison had sat at the feet of Donald Cargill and Richard Cameron, and had cast in her lot with them.

It was the cruelties perpetrated by the priests in Perth on the poor Covenanters that made her speak out. Instantly she was reported to the authorities for calling in question the conduct of the King's counsellors. A company of soldiers arrested her, and she joined Marion Harvey in Edinburgh.

When these two women were brought before the Privy Council, they had no charge to bring against the women. The Council seemed, however, to have come to that stage, that they were determined to shed blood just for the sake of shedding blood. They therefore set themselves to manufacture evidence against both women.

" Have you conversed with Donald Cargill ? " Bishop Paterson asked.

" I have seen him, and I wish that I had seen him oftener," answered Isabel Alison.

" Do you own the ' Sanquhar Declaration ? ' "

" Yes," answered both. " So long as the King held the truths of God, which he swore, we were obliged to own him ; but when he broke his oath, and robbed Christ of his Kingly Rights, which do not belong to the King, we were bound to disown and disobey him."

" Do you approve of the killing of Archbishop Sharp ? "

" In so far as God raised up instruments to execute His just judgments upon him, I have nothing to say against it ; for he was a perjured wretch, and a betrayer of the Kirk of Scotland."

With questions like these they tried to entrap the women, and got them to confess that they had talked often with Covenanters who had been outlawed by the

Government. The women refused to sign the evidence given, but the Council did it for them.

However, the evidence only became legal when delivered before the Justiciary Court. After a little delay the two women were taken there, and a long cross-examination took place. A packed jury were in their place, and the Crown lawyer, before the evidence was given, warned the jury that if they did not bring in the verdict as directed, they would be charged with a process of error.

The indictment is a very peculiar one. They were charged with receiving, maintaining, supplying, intercommuning and keeping correspondence with Donald Cargill, John Welsh, Richard Cameron. . . . . With owning the " Sanquhar Declaration," etc.

All the proof brought forward was the confession each had made.

" You know," said the infamous Sir George Mackenzie, " that these women are guilty of treason."

" It is not for treason but religion you are persecuting us," said Marion Harvey.

" It is not for religion but treason we are pursuing you," he retorted.

" It *is* for religion that you are pursuing us, and I am of the same religion that you have all sworn to be of. I am a true Presbyterian in my judgment."

The jury soon retired, and came with their verdict. Its rider, however, showed their temper.

" We find both guilty, in conformity with their confession of acknowledging the ' Sanquhar Declaration ' and the ' Bond of Combination '; but as actors or receptors of rebels, we find it not proven."

A minute was passed by the judges to delay sentence. At this Marion said:

" I charge you before the tribunal of God, as ye shall answer there; for ye have nothing to say against me but for my owning the persecuted gospel."

On the 21st of the month they were brought up for sentence. They knew their fate before they came.

" That ye be taken to the Grassmarket of Edinburgh, upon Wednesday, the 26th next, betwixt two and four o'clock in the afternoon, and there to be hanged on a gibbet till ye be dead, and all your lands, heritages, goods, and gear, whatsomever, to be escheat and inbrought to our Sovereign Lord's use, which was pronounced by doom."

Both of the women issued a confession from prison which is highly creditable to their Christian fortitude.

" Therefore let enemies and pretended friends say what they will," said Isabel Alison in her confession, " I could have my life on no easier terms than the denying of Christ's Kingly Office. So I lay down my life for owning and adhering to Jesus Christ, His being a free King in His own house, and I bless the Lord that ever He called me to that."

" And now I bless Him that thoughts of death are not terrible to me," said Marion Harvey. " He hath made me as willing to lay down my life for Him, as ever I was willing to live in the world. And now, ye that are His witnesses, be not afraid to venture on the Cross of Christ, for His yoke is easy and His burden light. It is my grief that I have not been more faithful for my Master, Christ. All His dealings with me have been in love and mercy. Oh, free love! I may say I am a brand plucked out of the fire; I am a limb of the devil plucked out from his fire-side. Oh, I am to wonder and admire at his condescending love."

According to the sentence they were brought to the Grassmarket to be executed. Here the last drop of bitterness was drunk, not in the death they endured, but in their companions in death. The Government, to make these two women appear odious to the world, hung five women with them who had been guilty of murdering their illegitimate children. It wounded their sense of delicacy, but with meekness they took this as part of the Cross they had to carry.

" Behold, I hear my Beloved saying unto me : ' Arise, my love, my fair one, and come away,' " said Marion Harvey, when going to death.

" Marion," said Bishop Paterson, " you said you would never hear a curate, now you shall be forced to hear one." And he called upon a curate to pray.

" Come, Isabel, let us sing the 23rd Psalm, " which they did, and the curate gave over his tirade against the Covenanters, which he called prayer.

Isabel Alison was the first to be hanged.

" Farewell, all created comforts ; farewell, sweet Bible, in which I delighted most, and which has been sweet to me since I came to prison ; farewell, Christian acquaintances. Now into Thy hands I commit my spirit, Father, Son, and Holy Ghost." At this the hangman turned her off the ladder—and she was dead.

Marion Harvey sung the 84th Psalm, and read the 3rd Chapter of Malachi. She then addressed the multitude around :

" I am come here to-day," she said, " for avowing Christ to be Head of His Church, and King in Zion. Oh, seek, sirs, seek Him, and ye shall find Him ; I sought Him, and found Him ; I held Him, and would not let Him go. Much of the Lord's presence I have enjoyed in prison ; and now I bless the Lord the snare is broken and we are escaped."

She then mounted the ladder and engaged in prayer.

" Oh, my fair one, my lovely one, come away," was heard, and she then became silent. After prayer she addressed the people again.

" I am not come here for murder, for they have no matter of fact to charge me with, but only my judgment. I am about twenty years of age. At fourteen I was a hearer of these curates and the Indulged ministers ; and while I was a hearer of these, I was a blasphemer and Sabbath-breaker, and a chapter of the Bible was a burden to me ; but since I heard this persecuted gospel, I durst not blaspheme nor break the Sabbath, and the Bible became my delight."

The multitude had broken into tears, and were evidently in deep sympathy with Marion. The provost feared the result if he allowed her to speak any more. He therefore gave the hangman the signal, and Marion Harvey was turned off the ladder before another word was spoken.

They were both buried in what was then called the "Traitor's Hole," in Greyfriars' Churchyard, Edinburgh. No doubt many traitors were buried there, but the bodies of holy men and women have made the place known to-day as " The Martyr's Grave."

A large tombstone has been erected to the honour of a hundred martyrs who have found a resting-place there.

" From May 27th, 1661, when the Noble Marquis of

Argyle was beheaded, to the 17th of February 1688, when James Renwick suffered, were, one way and another, murdered and destroyed for the same cause about eight-teen thousand, of whom were executed at Edinburgh about an hundred of Noblemen, Gentlemen, Ministers, and others; noble martyrs for Jesus Christ. The most of them lie here."

So reads the tombstone inscription. Several texts of Scripture are added, also a long poem.

"Be thou faithful unto death, and I will give thee a Crown of Life."—Revelation ii. 10.

IX.

ALEXANDER PEDEN, THE PROPHET.

THE strangest man of the Covenanting struggle was Alexander Peden. Around his name has grown a multitude of stories in which people have tried to express the wonderfulness of his character. Some of these stories are highly improbable. Yet in an age which believed in prophets having the power of foretelling things to come, these stories were accepted without much scrutiny. Laying aside such as have need of verification, we still have the picture of a strange man, spiritual in mind and heart, noble in character, keen of insight, and fully justified to the title which people gave him of " Prophet."

We must not deny the term, then, to Peden, because he died in his bed. This was not the fault of his enemies. To the hour of his death they hunted him, but failed to shed his blood.

Peden was a native of Ayrshire, being born at Auchencloich, in Sorn, about 1626. His father was a small proprietor, and left his eldest son a fair patrimony. His social position gave him an entrance into the best society, and we find him often at the Boswells of Auchinleck, and at the Baillies of Jerviswoode, and the houses of the gentry round about. From an early period he felt called to the ministry. The great difficulty of

such a career, through the deadness of religious life in
Scotland, and the trouble of getting hearts to receive
the Good News of Everlasting Life, weighed heavily upon
his spirit, and made him moody and sad. He, however,
went to the University and prepared himself for his life-
work, and in due time became pastor of New Luce, in
Galloway. It was a quiet place at the head of a narrow
glen, through which the Luce runs, breaking the stillness.

It was here the people first discovered he was a more
than ordinary man. His prayers were conversations
with a Personal Friend. His sermons were visions of
the glory of God which had come to him in his medita-
tions, and filled the people with awe. His talk was
about God and His will in regard to downtrodden Scotland. Tall in stature and well-built, as he proclaimed
his message of God he must have been intensely impressive.

His ministry here continued for three years, when the
" Drunken Act of Glasgow " compelled him, with several
hundred others, to leave his church. His people were
filled with the most intense sorrow, and when he had
preached his farewell sermon, they wept, and begged him
to preach on. The darkness of night came before the
congregation dispersed. He closed the pulpit door behind
him, and knocking it very hard with his Bible three
times, he said :

" In my Master's name I arrest thee ! that none enter
thee but as I have done—by the door."

As years passed and no attempt was made by those in
authority to fill up the vacancy, this action of Peden
became greatly talked about, and helped to increase his
fame.

He now took to preaching on the hillsides, and lived the life of a wanderer. He was afraid to sleep in the homes offered to him, for he knew the Council thirsted for his blood, and to be found in a house was to bring ruin upon it.

The Council, unable to capture him, issued a proclamation, charging him with holding conventicles at various places, and with baptizing children at Ralstoun, in Kilmarnock, and at Castlehill, in Cragie Parish. He was ordered to surrender himself, unconditionally, to the Council.

Instead of surrender, he joined the men implicated in the Pentland rising. He joined them at Lanark. To a man of his quick insight, the result of that rising was seen afar off.

" Ye are not ready for resistance," he told them, " and your present venture will end in defeat and worse persecution." And he left them. The Covenanters remembered his words when they were scattered by the Royalist troops. As, however, he had joined the Covenanters who fought at the Pentlands, Peden was included in the indictment issued against the leading insurgents. He again refused to appear before the Council, and was made an outlaw, and his property was forfeited to the Crown.

Peden's life was now one of great hardship, although he never was bothered by spies, as were many of the others. They feared his curse too much for that. Although they frequently knew where he slept, they kept silent, and he often wondered he was not taken.

Once whilst riding to a meeting with his friends, Mr Welch and the Laird of Glenover, he met a party of dragoons in search of himself. He boldly rode up to them, saying to his friends, "Keep up your courage and confidence, for God hath laid an arrest on these men that they shall do us no harm."

The soldiers inquired the road to a certain place, and Peden at once offered to show them the best place to ford the Titt. They were courtesy embodied, and thanked Peden profusely.

"I thought it better to go myself than send the lad," Peden explained to his friends. "They might have asked the lad awkward questions."

Not long after this, whilst hiding in Glendyne, he left his shelter and made for a cottage in the moorland, where he knew a godly man lived. He reached it safely, and was heartily welcomed and entertained by the old man. As was his custom, he held devotions at that house, and as sunset had come he returned to his dreary cave. In going along the path, he saw in front of him a company of dragoons. He fled across the moor, and passing one of the mountain burns, he saw a good hiding-place under an overhanging piece of bank. Into this he crept, and waited breathlessly for the coming of the troopers. As the horses came galloping along, they were compelled to leap the burn. In doing so the hoof of one of the horses pressed through the bank under which Peden lay, and grazed his head, pressing his bonnet deep into the soft clay. Praising God for his escape, he came out of his hiding place and went to his more comfortable cave.

Soon after this he made his way to Sanquhar, and hid above that ancient town. After a long fast, Peden and a few friends went over to Castle Gilmour and besought hospitality, which was readily granted.

They were sitting enjoying the good things laid before them, and talking about the things of the Kingdom of God, feeling free from danger, when they were startled by the sound of horses' hoofs. One of the company ran to the window and looked out, and saw a troop of dragoons preparing to dismount.

"Ye cannot hide here," said the master of Castle Gilmour, "nor can ye escape by the back." This was owing to the shape of the Castle.

"Let us rush out among the horses, waving our bonnets," said Peden, "and then escape by the loopholes in the court-yard wall."

It was no sooner said than put into force. The horses became so frightened that they reared and plunged, causing the soldiers to be more concerned about their own safety than the capture of Peden and his friends.

The fugitives rushed to a burn, and climbed its steep sides before the dragoons started after them. The nature of the ground made it impossible for the soldiers to follow.

The soldiers guessed that Peden and his companions would at once leave the district, and they went away in search of them. Peden, however, had agreed to hold a conventicle at the grey-clothed height of Auchengrouch. He lingered for this, and two days after his adventure the conventicle took place. Peden preached in his usual manner, to the joy of the people. The sermon was disturbed, however, by the appearance of a company of dragoons, who spread themselves over the hillside, determined to capture all who were there. Escape seemed impossible, and all eyes looked to Peden. They heard him beseech the protection of God. After prayer he said to them:

"Friends, the bitterest of this blast is over; we will be no more troubled with them this day."

This did not comfort them, however, and they begged that he should hide in some hole and they would cover him over with heather. He declined their offer, and asked them all to pray.

"Lord, we are ever needing at Thy hand, and if we had not Thy command to call upon Thee in the day of trouble, and Thy promise of answering us in the day of our distress, we wot not what would become of us. If Thou have any more work for us in Thy world, twine them about the hill, Lord, and cast the lap of Thy cloak over poor old Sandy and these people, and we will keep it in remembrance, and tell it to the commendation of Thy goodness, pity, and compassion, what Thou didst for us at such a time."

Dense white clouds of mist rose from the hillsides and enveloped the dragoons and Covenanters alike. As the latter saw the position of the dragoons and knew the hillside well, they at once went home through the mist. The dragoons dare not move a step, fearing danger. This incident raised Peden to a unique place in the hearts of the Covenanters, and from henceforth he was called "Peden, the Prophet."

The hunt after him, however, became so keen that he passed over to Ireland, and thereby ran into danger, for he was arrested in the house of Hugh Ferguson of Knockdow, in Carrick. He was taken to Edinburgh, brought before the Council, and sentenced to imprisonment in the Bass Rock. The sufferings of that period were very great, as those who have read the story of the "Martyrs of the Bass" can well testify.

There is a letter of Peden's extant, in which he thanks some friends for a contribution they had sent him.

"We are close shut up in our chambers; not permitted to converse, diet, or worship together; but conducted out by two at once in the day, to breathe in the open air—envying the birds their freedom, provoking and calling on us to bless Him for the most common mercies. Again, we are close shut up day and night, to hear only the sighs and groans of our fellow prisoners."

Peden suffered the trials of this life for five years, and he, with others, was then taken from the Bass and sentenced to perpetual banishment. America was to be their prison for the future. Peden, however, declared to his companions—on what grounds has never been discovered—that "the ship has not been built that would bear them over the sea to any of the plantations."

It added to their belief in him as a *prophet* when the whole company was released upon the arrival of the vessel at London. Peden lived in that city for a year, and then returned to Scotland. For the next five years he divided his time between Scotland and Ireland, or, as he called it, "between one bloody land and the other bloody land."

In 1682 we find him back preaching to his old congregation at Glen Luce. Some of those who heard him then have preserved these sermons.

"For you, the poor, broken-hearted followers of Christ, to whom He hath given grace to follow Him in the storm, I tell you, Grace is your glory. At your first conversion our Lord gives you the one end of the line but he keeps the other end in glory with Himself. But, sirs, He will have you all there at length.

" Where is the Church of God in Scotland, sirs, at this
day ?   It is not amongst the great clergy.   I will tell
you where the Church is.   It is wherever a praying
young man or young woman is at a dykeside in Scotland ; that's where the Church is.   A praying party
shall go through the storm.   But many of you in this
countryside know not these things.   The weight of the
broken Church of Scotland never troubles you.   The
loss of a cow, or an ill market-day, goes nearer your
hearts than all the troubles of the Church of God.   Poor
creature that resolvest to follow Him, pray fast !   If
there be one of you, He will be the second ; if there be
two, He will be a third.   Ye shall never want company."

Although only sixty years of age, he knew his race
was run.   He returned to his old home at Auchencloich,
only to find the dragoons searching for him.   He lived,
therefore, in a cave, and spent his days in prayer.

" It is a praying Church we need to-day.   I am done
with preaching.   Carry me to Ayr's Moss, and bury me
beside Ritchie, that I may have rest in my grave, for I
have had little in my life.   Na, na ; bother not where ye
lay me, for my body will be lifted again."   Which was
soon verified.

He came from his cave to his brother's home.   The
dragoons were hovering about, and his sister-in-law
feared they would come and find him.

" They will not find me alive though they search
twenty times this house."   Next day he was dead.

The Boswells of Auchinleck interred Peden in their
private vaults, to save his body from insult.   But it was
only for a time.   The dragoons heard where Peden was

buried, and broke into the grave. His body was carried to Cumnock, and hung on the gibbet in chains. The Countess of Dumfries interceded with the Council, and Peden's body was buried at the foot of the gibbet. In honour to Peden, others desired to be buried beside him. The foot of the gallows thus became the popular burial-ground and the recognised churchyard of Cumnock. A thorn bush was planted at his head and another at his feet.

None of the martyrs was so revered by the people as Peden. His acts were considered judgments of God, and he predicted so many things that came to pass, that he was linked with Moses, Isaiah, and Jeremiah in greatness. He was one of the comforters of the poor Covenanters, and bravely shared their privations. His name became sacred, and all those who had shown kindness to him praised God for this honour.

X.

JAMES RENWICK.

THE Government were ill advised when they determined to hang the saintly Donald Cargill in the Grassmarket, Edinburgh. Instead of striking terror in the hearts of those who beheld such cruelty, it kindled such a fire in one soul, that from that time a new force swayed the Covenanters.

No one would have suspected there was any possibility of that white-faced youth, that stood not far from the gallows, turning a leader of the Covenanters. His large blue eyes, white pinched face, fair hair, showed he was delicate in body, but the tight compression of his lips showed the force of his soul. This youth was James Renwick. Cargill's dying words made the tears burst from his eyes; and there, in the presence of death, he vowed his life should be spent in the cause that had received the support of such a godly man as Donald Cargill.

James Renwick came of poor parentage, his father being a weaver at Minniehive, in Nithsdale. He was the only son spared to them, and, with true Scotch piety, they gave him to the Lord.

As a child he was precocious, and seemed to endure doubts and fears at twelve years of age that are only possible to others of a maturer growth. He was passionately fond of reading, and through the assistance of well-wishers he was sent to Edinburgh University.

His knowledge of God, and the things of God, was only obtained after hard mental warfare.

"If these hills," he once said, "were all-devouring furnaces of burning brimstone, I should be content to go through them all if so be I could be assured there was a God."

Peace came to him, as it ever does to the *honest* seeker after God. He was now prepared to assure others, having been assured himself.

Now that he had put his hand to the plough, he was amazed to find how much there was to do. Herds of people went to the Episcopal Church to listen to the ignorant babblings of men who had been taken from the fields and put into the pulpit. He was disappointed when he saw how the people acquiesced in this. And his mind was filled with torment when he heard the ousted ministers plead for compromise.

"When God's heritage is being ravined by wolves, is this the hour for compromise?" he said indignantly at one of their meetings. "It is better to lay one's life down, as Donald Cargill did, and let the world see what we mean, than temporise and betray God and His people. We must be thorough or nothing; and, as for me, from this day my life is the Lord's. Let Him do to me what seemeth Him good."

He immediately came to the front as the organiser of the Covenanting party. He consented to the Declaration which sanctioned war against the reigning sovereign, on the ground of the King being the enemy of religion, liberty, and all true government. He denied that magistrates had any powers but those given them by the people and for the people.

" Magistrates have no power but what is derived from the people ; and magistrates have nothing actually, but what the people have virtually ; yea, and more than virtually, for they may actually confer it upon whom they think fit. For the power of government is natural and radical to them, being unitedly in the whole, and singularly in every one of them. So, whatever a magistrate may do, the people may do the same, either wanting magistrates, or the magistrates failing or refusing to do their duty."

The Covenanters realised that a prince had been born in their midst, and all eyes were upon Renwick. As he would not take the oath of supremacy at Edinburgh University, he was refused his degree, and his theological education was suddenly stopped. The Societies, however, agreed to send him to Holland, and he went to the University of Gottingen. His time of training was very short, for he was back again in Scotland in six months' time.

During those six months his heart was more occupied with the state of affairs in Scotland than with his studies. Letter after letter brought him news of cruelty, oppression, and martyrdom.

" My longings and earnest desires to be in Scotland, with that pleasant remnant, are very great. I cannot tell what may be in it, but I hope the Lord hath either some work to work, or else is minded presently to call for a testimony at my hand ; and if He give me frame and furniture, I desire to welcome either of them.

MONUMENT AT STIRLING TO THE WIGTOWN MARTYRS.

Courage yet! for all that is come and gone. The loss
of men is not the loss of the Cause. What is the
matter though we all fall? The Cause shall not fall.
Let us be lions in God's cause and lambs in our own."

The Covenanters' greatest foe was the spy that crept
into their midst. These men came openly to the meetings, even although they were suspected, believing that
the Covenanters would never use force. Renwick
determined to deal with these men, and with the
assaults that the dragoons made on their meetings, by
making a declaration in which he said that, in self-
defence, they would resist dragoon and spy.

" Let not any think that (our God assisting us) we
will be so slack-handed in time coming to put matters
into execution as heretofore we have been, seeing we
are bound faithfully and valiantly to maintain our
Covenants and the cause of Christ. Therefore, let all
persons be admonished of their hazard ; and particularly,
all ye spies, who, by your voluntary information, endeavour to render us up into the enemy's hands, that
our blood may be shed. Sinless necessity for self-
preservation, accompanied with holy zeal for His reigning in our land, and suppressing of profanity, will move
us not to let you pass unpunished. Call to remembrance
all that is in peril is not lost, and all that is delayed is
not forgiven."

The rise of the Covenanters, under the inspiration of
Renwick, filled the Government with consternation.
He seemed to be in all parts of Scotland at once, his
movements were so speedy. He always had a fleet horse,
bridled and ready, when he preached; on the first signal
of alarm he was off like the wind.

H

A price was fixed upon his head, and no one, under the penalty of death, was to give him shelter, a morsel of bread, a cup of cold water, to talk with, or even salute him. He was constantly beset by spies and soldiers, and at times found it hard to escape.

He had arranged to hold a conventicle at Blagannoch, a large stretch of moss-hags in the very heart of the mountains, between Sanquhar and Muirkirk. It was impossible to get there on horse-back, so he walked the twenty miles in the night-time. His meetings had been broken up so often that the greatest secrecy was observed. As he had no horse, and being very delicate in body, some stratagem had to be adopted to save his life if the dragoons came.

Mr Laing, of Blagannoch, agreed to exchange clothes with Renwick, and so to decoy the soldiers after the wrong man. Laing knew every inch of the mountain so well, he was certain he could escape.

The people sat down on the heather, and a tent was lifted up to shield Renwick should it rain. His text was, " He that toucheth you, toucheth the apple of His eye." In the midst of the sermon a messenger was seen hurrying as fast as possible to the meeting-place.

" Ye are betrayed, my friends, and the enemy is at hand."

All was confusion in a moment. Several of Renwick's friends took his hand and hurried him away from the spot. Laing, in his assumed clerical attire, awaited the approach of the dragoons. The moment their eyes rested upon him, they gave a shout. They now felt sure Renwick was in their power. But Laing, taking an opposite direction from what Renwick had taken, plunged into the morass. Following a sheep-track, he led the soldiers on in pursuit. The horses did well for a time, but at last they began to sink and a halt was called. It was then agreed that a few should follow the fugitive on foot. But the weight of their armour soon made it impossible for them to follow, they sank so deeply into the morass. The scream of one of the soldiers who had fallen into a hole arrested the others. The soldier had broken his leg. The misfortune of their comrade absorbed their attention, and Laing got away.

Renwick's many escapes made him at times inclined to court danger, as the following story will show:

Whilst arranging to hold a conventicle in the wilds of lower Galloway, he went to stay at the house of a trusted follower, who kept an inn. To the dismay of both, a company of dragoons rode up to the door and informed the innkeeper they would stay there that night.

Fortunately, Renwick had a rough suit of tweeds on at that time and was not identified, but talked with the soldiers. They were not slow to express their feelings about the Covenanters, and especially Renwick.

" There's to be a conventicle somewhere about here, and we intend to hold him tight this time. We know not, however, where it is to be."

" I think," said Renwick in a whisper, " I can help you in the pinch."

" Indeed," said the officer, " that will be a good service, for I am tired hunting him."

" Then keep your mind easy on the matter, and not a whisper to anyone. I plight you my word that by to-morrow at this time Renwick's hand will be in yours."

" Take this as reward for your offer," said the officer,
placing some coins in Renwick's hand.

The landlord said nothing, but wondered whatever
Renwick could mean. He understood everything when
he spoke privately to Renwick before retiring for the
night.

Seated on a horse that Renwick was supposed to
have borrowed from the innkeeper, he, chatting with
the officer, led the way to the conventicle. The six
soldiers got their guns ready, and looked forward to great
slaughter and the reward for Renwick's head.

" It will be impossible for horses to go the rest of the
journey," said Renwick dismounting, and soon the horses
were tied to trees.

The place of meeting was in the bosom of two hills, a
kind of basin that had been scooped out by nature. It
was a place where a thousand persons could meet and be
unobserved. Only those who knew the place could find it.

" We'll go down this side," said Renwick, and the eight
men were speedily sliding down the hill. Soon the people
came in sight, but though they must have seen the
dragoons, they heeded not. One that looked like the
minister stood at the far end of the assembly.

" Take Renwick and slay every man that hinders
you," said the officer.

It was a time of suspense for the congregation, and
one of anxiety for Renwick.

As the soldiers turned behind a huge boulder twenty-
four guns were levelled at them.

" Drop your guns or we fire," came the order, and
the officer saw resistance was useless. Being disarmed,
Renwick turned to the officer.

" The promise I made you is fulfilled. Come up to
the preaching place, and I will put your hand into that
of James Renwick."

When the two were arrived at the preaching-desk,
Renwick addressed the congregation.

" Our enemy here wished to put his hand into that of
James Renwick. He hath even paid me to do him this
service. I do him the service, but return his money. I
am James Renwick, sir," he said, addressing the officer.

" James Renwick ! impossible, a man so harmless, so
discreet, and so well informed ; if you are James Renwick,
I, for one, will pursue you no longer."

And with peculiar feelings of gratitude to God the
conventicle was held, the soldiers having a prominent
place assigned them.

It was in Balmacellan, in Galloway, the following
incident took place :

Renwick had sent round word to the Covenanters that
he wished to hold a meeting. He only sent to those
whom he thought he could trust ; but one of them
betrayed him. As the service was about to commence
the dragoons appeared. They surrounded the people,
and escape was only possible by crossing the river above
Dalry. But the flooded state of the river made this
very risky. Before they entered its seething waters,
they kneeled by the river side and prayed. As they
rose from their knees they saw the troopers on the other
side of the river. In their desire to capture Renwick
they had let the others escape, and had followed hard
after him.

Leaving the water-side he sought a place of shelter.
Drawing near to a cottage he heard the sound of singing

and thought that he had stumbled upon some godly hearts. He knocked at the door, and to his disgust found a company of shepherds drinking. He was, with Scotch hospitality, welcomed in, and food laid before him.

The good lady of the house suspected he was a Covenanter, and took him away early to rest. In the morning he was sore perplexed to find his clothes had disappeared. He suspected betrayal, and looked about for any garments to put on. His fears were soon allayed by the voice of the good woman of the house, who heard he was up.

" Your claithes are sae weet they're no dry yet. Here's my guid man's plaid that 'ill dae for a coat. The rest is dry, but no your coat."

He sat down to breakfast with a thankful heart, and after partaking of it he asked the household to join in devotion, which they did.

He was standing at the door, inhaling the hot air, when a company of dragoons came in sight. It was useless to run, for he could not escape. He coaxed one of the dogs with him, and he determined to go and meet the dragoons, trusting to his shepherd's plaid for a disguise.

" Are you the master of that cottage ? " asked the officer.

" No, but you'll find him busy in that field there," he said, pointing to where some sheep were being fed.

" You've seen no fugitives on this side of the water, have you ? "

" No, I've seen none. The water is very heavy, and cannot be crossed." And with that they were satisfied, and left him. He instantly went back to the house, got dressed, and started for the place where he had arranged to meet some of his friends.

He was deeply impressed by his escape at this time, and used often to refer to it.

RENWICK'S ENCOUNTER WITH THE TROOPERS.

"My business," he writes in one of his letters, "was never so weighty, so multiplied, and so ill to be guided, to my apprehension, as it hath been this year; and my body was never so frail. Excessive travel, night-wanderings,

unseasonable sleep and diet, and frequent preaching in
all seasons of weather, especially in the night, have so
debilitated me, that I am often incapable for any work.
I find myself greatly weakened inwardly, so that I
sometimes fall into fits of swooning and fainting. When
I use means for my recovery, I find it someways effectual;
but my desire to the work, and the necessity and impor-
tunity of people, prompt me to do more than my natural
strength will well allow, and to undertake such toilsome
business as casts my body presently down again. I
mention not this through any anxiety, quarrelling, or
discontents, but to show you my condition in this
respect. I may say that, under all my frailties and
distempers, I find great peace and sweetness in reflecting
upon the occasion thereof. It is part of my glory and
joy to bear such infirmities, contracted through my
poor and small labour in my Master's vine-yard."

It is a catalogue of woes, this, that reminds us of the
apostle Paul's. His zeal in the work of God was eating
him up. His sermons became more personal, and of a
highly spiritual stamp.

"Count the cost of religion. God is a liberal Leader;
deal not niggardly with Him. Lay down to Him your
names, your enjoyments, your lives, your all at His
feet, for He only is worthy to have the disposal of them;
and the sufferings of this present time are not worthy
to be compared with the glory that shall be revealed.
Think not much to quit the vain and carnal delights of
this world; they cannot satisfy your senses, much less
your souls. The earth is round, the heart of man is
three-cornered; therefore, *this* cannot be filled with *that*.
And though ye could find content in them, yet how vain

were it because inconstant, and how unsolid because how uncertain."

Had not the hand of the enemy been laid upon Renwick, he most certainly would have burnt out, he worked so unceasingly.

It was in January 1688 Renwick came to Edinburgh, to deliver into the hands of the Moderator a protest he intended to issue against the Presbyterians accepting Indulgence from the Crown.

Having done this he crossed over to Fife to hold meetings there, and at the end of the month he came back to Edinburgh. Here he usually lodged with one named John Lookup, a dealer in English goods. Although a staunch friend of Renwick's he was suspected of dealing in contraband goods, and his premises were frequently searched.

It happened that Thomas Justice, an officer, heard singing in the house of Lookup, and at once suspected that Renwick was inside. He waited until the morning, and with a company of searchers came to Lookup's house. Renwick, hearing a noise, went to the door, when Justice exclaimed :

" My life for it, this is James Renwick. All within this house must go to the guard that they may show what trade they are of."

" I shall soon show you what is my trade," said Renwick in a determined manner. This so terrified Justice that he rushed into the street calling upon all and sundry to assist him in the capture of " that dog Renwick."

Meanwhile, Renwick had armed himself, and hastened to another door. Here a great crowd confronted him. Seizing his pistol he fired it in the air, and instantly the

crowd parted. He rushed through the middle of it, and
was just outside the mob, when a man struck him on the
chest with a stick. Renwick reeled and would have
fallen, but a woman gave him assistance. He could not
run, however, owing to the pain, and he swooned. Re-
covering, he got on his legs again, only to find a mob
coming after him, headed by Justice. The shouts of
Justice attracted attention, and some men enclosed
Renwick, and he was arrested.

He was taken at once to the guard-house, and became
exposed to the insults of those there.

"What!" cried Graham, the captain of the guard;
"is this *boy* the James Renwick that the whole nation
has been so troubled with?"

His sensitive nature and highly strung temperament
made him shudder at the torture which he dreaded was
before him.

"How shall I endure to have these hands struck off,
and my legs tortured in the boots, and my head taken
off my body?" And then he threw himself upon the
floor and agonised with God that the cruelties of his
enemies might be so far restrained as to do nothing
against him beside taking his life.

He was brought before some members of the Council,
who were astonished at the youthful and delicate appearance of Renwick. They questioned him about his
principles, and after the examination Viscount Tarbet
said to Chancellor Perth:

"He is the stiffest maintainer of his principles that
ever came before us. Others we used always to cause,
one time or other, to waver; but him we could never
move. Where we found him, there we left him. We

could never make him yield or vary in the least. He is of old Knox's principles."

After a great delay his mother was allowed to see him.

" How shall I look upon that head and these hands set up among the rest on the port of the city."

" I have offered my life unto the Lord, and have sought that He may bind them up, and I am persuaded that they shall not be permitted to torture my body, nor touch one hair of my head further. The terror of torture, however, is so far removed, that I would rather be cast into a cauldron of boiling oil than do anything to wrong truth."

Soon his indictment was laid into his hands. He was charged with denying the King's authority, refusing to pay the war-tax, and counselling his followers to come with arms to the field-meetings.

" I own all authority which has its prescriptions and limitations from the Word of God ; but cannot own this usurper as lawful King, seeing, both by the Word of God, such a one is incapable to bear rule, and also by the ancient laws of the kingdom, which admit none to the Crown of Scotland until he swear to defend the Protestant religion, which a man of his confession cannot do.

" Would it have been thought lawful for the Jews, in the days of Nebuchadnezzar, each to bring a coal to augment the flame of the furnace to devour the three children, if they had been so required by the King? And how can it be right to pay a war-tax which is to oppress my brethren ?

" I own I taught them to carry arms to defend themselves, and to resist the acts of violence perpetrated by your command and under your authority."

His sentence was ready before he entered the Court, and, notwithstanding his able defence, he was found guilty, and sentenced to be executed in three days.

"Prisoner, do you desire longer than three days?" asked the Justice-General.

"It is all one to me.   If protracted, it is welcome; if shortened, it is welcome.   My Master's time is the best."

Then a wondrous thing happened.   His jail was hourly besieged by the Bishop of Edinburgh, the King's advocate, the nobility of Edinburgh and district, beseeching Renwick to apply for pardon.   He resisted all their entreaties, however, and at last the Bishop left him, saying: "It was a pity he had been of such principles, for he was a pretty lad."

To the Romish priests who came to see him, Renwick had but one word—"Begone!"

On the morning of his execution he wrote many letters.

"The Lord hath been wonderfully gracious to me since I came to prison.   He hath assured me of His salvation, helped me to give a testimony for Him, and own before His enemies all that I have taught, and strengthened me to resist and repel many temptations and assaults," he wrote to one friend.

When he came to the place of execution on the 17th February 1688, he was calm and collected.   The drums beat during the time he tried to speak to the people.   " I shall soon be above these clouds—I shall soon be above these clouds; then shall I enjoy Thee and glorify Thee, O my Father, without interruption and without intermission for ever.   Death to me is as a bed to the weary."   And he was not, for God took him.

The extreme position Renwick took was legalised in the November of this same year, when William of Orange came to this country. " The death of men is not the death of the Cause," said Renwick once. His death accelerated the triumph of his cause. The crimes he was charged with, and for which he gave up his life, were legalised as Rights within one year of his execution.

He was the last of the heroes of the Scottish Covenant, and one of the youngest. He never looked more than a boy of eighteen, although he was twenty-six when executed. His life was the last required in the gaining of liberty of conscience and freedom in religion. He grudged it not, but counted himself honoured in being a martyr for the Lord Jesus Christ.

> " Thy persecuted children, Scotia, foiled
> A tyrant and a bigot's bloody laws.
> There, leaning on his spear,
> The lyart veteran heard the Word of God
> By Cameron thundered, or by RENWICK poured
> In gentle streams ; then rose the long, the loud
> Acclaim of praise. The wheeling plover ceased
> His plaint, the solitary place was glad,
> And on the distant cairn the watcher's ear
> Caught, doubtfully at times, the breeze-borne note."

XL

SOME HEROINES OF THE COVENANT.

In all the great movements that have been for the good of the world, woman has never shirked bearing her share of the agony which the birth of every truth or liberty entails. The reason the world is so full of the truth of God to-day, and that we have so many liberties, is, that woman is ever ready to endure hardship and suffering patiently.

The greatness of her self-sacrifice has not always been seen, for she seldom scales the heights of battle. Heroism is not seen to advantage, however, in the battle-charge, when the manhood is too often overruled by baser feelings. It is the long, dreary, weary march that tries the true spirit of the soldier, and reveals the stuff that heroes are made of.

Because no woman led the Covenanters into battle, or wrote out a declaration, or preached on the hillside at the risk of her life, we must not imagine there were no other ways in which heroism could display itself. Woman has sent her martyrs to the gallows, given her witnesses to be shot on the lonely hillside, lived in caves and dens of the earth, and suffered untold agonies that only are known to God.

At the back of the whole Covenanting movement,

helping to keep it healthy and pure, and full of sane guiding-power, was the heroic love and endurance of woman. Whilst woman's natural appeal to man's better nature saved her from some of the cruelties the soldiers practised on men, yet no one can read about the sufferings and sorrows and anxieties of the wives of the Covenanters without blushing at man's inhumanity to woman.

There is an agony of the heart and mind keener far than that of physical suffering. If you wish to understand this, read carefully the story of Mrs William Veitch. It is a life full of trial and tribulation, borne with the noblest Christian fortitude. Yet, although she might have chosen an easier life had she desired it, her one ambition was to assist her husband in carrying out what he considered to be his duty to God.

Mr Veitch, her husband, had joined the Covenanters owing to the cruelties of the troopers of Sir James Turner. He was at the Pentland rising, and had to flee for his life. Mrs Veitch tramped with him in the night-time into England, and then returned to her home at the Westhills of Dunsyre. She had not long returned home before the troopers began to visit her house.

" Where is your rogue of a husband ? " asked a trooper.

" My husband is no rogue, but an honest, God-fearing man. He is now safe in England," Mrs Veitch said spiritedly.

" And you helped him there, I'm told. I'll have to take you to prison."

" With me you can do what is your duty. I am ready to do mine."

One of the troopers suggested she was untruthful, and that no doubt her husband was hiding in the house

They consequently began to examine the house. They stabbed the beds with their swords, and ruined the beds. They threw dishes and household utensils on the middle of the floor. Religious books were thrown into the fire, whilst the meal and potatoes and hams, the staple food of the family, were destroyed in front of her door. Whatever was of value they carried away. This plundering left her in great poverty, which was increased by the soldiers returning every other day and ransacking the house again.

At the instigation of her husband she removed to Edinburgh, and then went to him at Stantonhall, in the parish of Longhoosly.

His enemies did not allow him peace for long, however, for they tried to arrest him. Two Justices of the Peace broke into his house, and with loaded pistols commanded Mrs Veitch to declare where her husband was. Naturally a timid woman, the sight of the pistols terrified her. The thought of her husband made her brave, however, and she declined to tell his hiding place. The Justices then laid hold of her, and threatened to beat her with sticks unless she told where her husband was.

" You are at liberty to beat this frail body if it gives you satisfaction. Pain is not a cheerful thing to bear, but the Lord Jesus will certainly give me all needed grace," she said quietly, and they left her.

Some months later a company of dragoons broke into their house at five o'clock in the morning, and found Mr Veitch enjoying his own bed. They at once arrested him, to the great grief of Mrs Veitch.

" It bred some trouble and new fear to my spirit," she writes in her diary, " but God was graciously pleased to set home that word, 'He does all things well. Trust in the Lord, and fear not what man can do,' which brought peace to me in such a measure that I was made often to wonder; for all the time the officers were in the house, God supported me, so that I was not the least discouraged before them."

The twelve days her husband lay in Morpeth jail were days of great bitterness of soul. Her life was particularly wrapped up in that of her husband, and with a woman's keen sympathy she was suffering with him. The fact that the Government had mentioned Mr Veitch's name as a rebel in one of their proclamations filled her mind with distress, for scarce a day passed but news of some Covenanter being done to death reached her. Those who had fought by Mr Veitch's side at the Pentland rising had been put to death, and she greatly feared the same fate was in store for him.

As each day passed and no decision had been made, the pain of anxiety became very intense.

Of this period she writes: "I was under much exercise of mind, which made me go to God many times on behalf of my husband. He made that word often sweet to me, 'He performeth the things appointed for me! He is of one mind, and who can turn Him?' Misbelief made me fearful in heart, for I was a stranger in a strange land, and had six small children, and little in the world to look to. But He comforted me with these words :

> " ' Oh, why art thou cast down, my soul,
> What should discourage thee?
> And why with vexing thoughts art thou
> Disquieted in me?'"

I

On her husband being sent to Scotland, she rode to Morpeth through a great snowstorm to see him. She saw him for a little time, and then returned to her children, having one upon the breast.

" I was in much exercise about him," she writes, " and it was my prayer to God, who I can say is a present help in the time of trouble, that he might be kept from the evil of sin ; which God was graciously pleased to answer."

The yearning of her heart for her dear husband made her start for Edinburgh in the depth of winter, leaving her children in the care of a friend. She arrived in the capital only to hear sentence of death passed on him. This seemed to be contrary to all her ideas of God's assurances to her, yet her hope was in God. And in July her husband was liberated, and " we came both home in peace to our children, where we lived at Stantonhall, three miles from Morpeth."

It requires little imagination to feel how deeply this saintly woman suffered. The passionate love she had for her husband made every calamity that befell him a source of sorrow to her. At times she was reduced to beggary, owing to the spoiling of her goods by the soldiers, and her husband's absence. Yet with boldness she remained faithful to her God, and suffered with her husband as a witness for Jesus Christ.

A story of an equally brave woman is that of Mrs Wilson of Durisdeer.

Her husband was famed for his piety, and therefore became a fit subject for persecution. Learning the intention of the dragoons to arrest him, he imparted the upsetting news to his wife,

" Where you go, I go, and in your hardships I am by your side," she said, and lifting her child, the three proceeded to a cave in one of the dark linns of Enterkin. The cave could only be entered by climbing down the face of a steep rock, but once entered, it was impregnable. It was well for them that this was so, for they had scarcely entered it before the soldiers were upon them. They began to fire at the cave's mouth with the hope of killing them, but fortunately none of the bullets took effect. One of the soldiers, therefore, offered to climb down to the cave, and engage Wilson in single combat. Mrs Wilson saw the soldier hanging on by the brushwood, and in an instant divined his object.

" We are in the hands of God, my love," she said to her husband, who was deeply concerned about the fate of his wife and child.

" I have no wish to shed blood, but if he ventures into the mouth of the cave I will fire," said Wilson, getting his gun ready. The soldier swung himself into the cave, and fired at random. Wilson returned the fire, and the soldier rolled down the face of the rocks into the burn beneath, dead.

The soldiers now determined to starve out the dauntless Covenanters. Mrs Wilson kept a cheerful heart, although the water had soaked all their clothes. She hugged her babe to her breast to keep it warm, and the long weary hours of the night passed on.

Wilson, however, determined to give the soldiers the slip in the dead of night, if possible. He removed his boots from his feet, and asked his wife to do likewise. After carefully picking the most suitable moment, when the men were sheltering under the trees owing to a heavy fall of rain, Wilson took his babe into his arms, and assisting his wife, they stealthily crept along the steep and dangerous bank. A slip and they would be hurled down into the torrent beneath. No misfortune overtook them, and, to the dismay of the soldiers, in the morning the cave was empty. They wandered up and down the countryside for some time after this, but eventually came back to their home in peace.

The wife of James Nivison was a woman of an equally noble spirit. Mr Nivison had shown his piety by attending the hill-meetings at the risk of his life. Although several times chased by the dragoons, he had always escaped them. He was sought for so persistently, however, that he never dared venture home. He wrote his wife several tender letters, which have been preserved.

" God will be with us both, with me in the wilderness and with you in the house, in which, though solitary, you shall not be alone. In removing for a season I will thereby provide both for your safety and my own."

She was not satisfied, however, with this arrangement. For her to abide at home and enjoy its comfort, and her husband to sleep by the side of rivers, or amongst the wet moss-hags, was not to her liking.

" I will go with you," she wrote to him, " and if the archers should hit you, I will be present to staunch your wounds and to bind up your bleeding head; in whatever danger you may be in, I will be at your side, your affectionate wife in life or death." And she followed him with a babe in her arms.

Through the day they hid on the hill-tops or in the dense woods. At night they found shelter under the overhanging banks of the streams or in caves.

The father made a cradle of willows for the little child, and when they removed from one place to another, its little wicker bed was carried also.

They had many terrible hours of anxiety when soldiers happened to draw near. Once their baby nearly betrayed them by its crying. The soldiers heard the screams, and made for the place where the fugitives were hiding. Fortunately the mother managed to quieten the child, and the soldiers failed to find the hiding-place.

The lack of food was one of the severest trials the mother had to endure. At times, owing to the proximity of the dragoons, the fugitives could not go to the farmhouses and beg for food.

For two years they wandered about, enduring the greatest hardships. When they returned to their home, it was to find it in ruins. All their goods had been destroyed. Yet they took all these trials meekly, counting it a great honour to suffer thus for the Lord Jesus Christ.

A large number of the wives of the Covenanters had to manifest their heroism in another manner. Hundreds of the Covenanters were torn from their families, put on board vessels and sent abroad. Their wives were not allowed to share the banishment of their husbands. To be parted by the grave is bitter, but it is inevitable. This was a parting worse than the grave, for it was a cruelty that ought never to have been allowed.

The story of Mrs John Mathison of Rosehill can be taken as an illustration, although her case has some favourable points in it not found in the story of others.

John Mathison was a great friend of the venerable Peden, and well known as an attender at conventicles, the penalty for which was death.

For a time he eluded his enemies, but at last, through the treachery of an informer, he was caught, and eventually banished to the island of New Jersey.

Mrs Mathison pleaded to be allowed to go with him, but her request was refused. To part from her husband, for what seemed to be ever, in this unnatural manner caused her intense sorrow. The children around her knee were unprovided for, and she would have to take the father's place. To bear such agony of soul for righteousness was indeed a great trial.

"God is above us and will be our hope and stay in this dark hour of tribulation. If we meet not on earth we will meet at the Master's right hand, no more to be parted," he said to his wife.

"It is a great price the Lord has asked this day, but I pay it for His glory. When I took Him for my Lord, I remembered what He suffered for me. I count it all joy He has made us partakers of His sufferings."

The tears flowed amidst the good confession. He tenderly took leave of his wife and his children, and was hurried off to the vessel.

Her heart went across the sea to her husband. Weary months came and went without a message ever being exchanged, and her hair grew grey through sorrow.

It is pleasing to relate that after some years he was able to return to his native land. He was so changed his wife knew him not. One of his sons recognised him, however, and said to his mother:

"If my father be alive, this is certainly he."

And in the joy of their reunion they tried to forget all the sorrows they had endured in the service of God their Father.

A story of a different nature from the one above is that of Mrs Howatson. It is one, however, that displays all the nobility and grandeur of the heroine's spirit.

Her husband's attachment to the Covenanting cause made it impossible for him to remain at home during the daytime. At night he crept home, and received a loving welcome from his wife. Her joy at his presence was often turned into fear when the soldiers thundered at their door in the dead of night.

At one of these times she awoke and saw four men standing before the peat fire trying to blow it into a flame. Without uttering a word, she aroused her husband, and with nothing but a white sheet to protect him, he fled past the men like a dart. They fired at him, but no shot took effect, to the gladness of his wife. With great risk she took him food and clothing in the early morning.

Once the dragoons entered her home when she was in bed with her baby one day old. They at once began to abuse and threaten her with punishment unless she revealed the hiding-place of her husband. They turned the house upside down, and even stabbed the bed on which she lay, with their swords, to her great terror, for she expected every moment that her babe would be killed.

" In God is my hope and salvation. I will fear no evil, for Thou art with me," she kept repeating to herself. " I will not reveal where my husband hides from your cruel and bloody swords," she said boldly.

They then laid hold of her little boy, and dragged him from the room. His screams tore the mother's heart, for she was unable to go to his protection.

The child was taken to a hill top, and tied to a tree,

and then they nearly made him frantic by threatening to kill him with their swords. The plan they had adopted to find the hiding-place of Howatson succeeded, for, on hearing the screams of his child, he rushed from the cave.

At once they laid hold of him, and the grief of knowing that her husband was captured was added to the others she suffered.

During the night the soldiers became drunk, and Howatson escaped.

"I knew that the Lord would not refuse this my petition on your behalf," she said, when her husband told her about his capture and escape.

For weeks after Howatson's escape his wife had to endure great hardships owing to the wantonness and cruelty of the soldiers. Meekly she bore their insults, with great fortitude she endured the spoiling of her goods, and boldly she spoke to them of God, to whom vengeance belongeth. She was a woman of whom the world was not worthy, and Scotland suffered a distinct loss when she and her equally estimable husband went to Ireland.

It required very little in those days to bring persecution upon one's head.

Mrs James Guthrie was found with a copy of a book which defended her husband's life and work in her possession. She had neither written the book, nor assisted to disseminate it. It had been sent to her by the author. Yet she was immediately brought before the Council, and, although there was no law against the book then, she was condemned to leave Edinburgh and make her home in cold bleak Shetland.

A COVENANTERS' COMMUNION.

In the Parish of Auchinleck, Mary Howie refused to take an oath abjuring the Covenanting principles. Immediately the soldiers lit a fire and began to burn her fingers until the bones were bare and black. This was a cruelty frequently perpetrated.

The story of Marion Cameron, sister to Richard Cameron, is one of melancholy interest. Like her brother, she was famed for her piety, and constantly attended the hill meetings. At one of these the soldiers came upon them, and the Covenanters fled like hunted partridges. Marion and two others fled towards Daljig, and hid among the moss-hags.

When they were safe from pursuit, as they thought, they began to sing some of the psalms to cheer their hearts. It happened a soldier heard their singing, and immediately called to one or two of his comrades, and they surrounded the worshippers.

" If ye burn your Bibles before us we will spare your lives," said the leader of the soldiers.

" Rather than so blaspheme God by such an act, we would give our lives a hundred times were that possible," was their reply.

" Then you shall have the pleasure of giving your life once at least," said the sergeant. " Ye are cursed rebels, and ought to die for your lack of allegiance to the King."

" We are not rebels," said Marion, fearlessly. " The King hath not more obedient servants than we are in all things that pertain to a king's affairs. We cannot obey the King if he comes between us and God."

" Ye will get plenty of time in heaven to worship your God, who seems to take little care of you," said the sergeant, with a laugh. He gave instant orders for his soldiers to fire, and Marion's blood stained the heather.

After some days they were found dead, and the three bodies were buried where they had fallen, witnessing for God.

The records of the period give a multitude of instances of women who were heroines in the truest sense. Large numbers were banished from the country. Others were burned on the cheek, and then allowed to remain in their native country. Heavy fines were inflicted on women who had means. Crimes that cannot be named were frequently done by the half-drunken soldiers. Many died in the caves and dens of the earth, and were never more heard about. Others took colds and died as the result of what they had to suffer. On the lonely hillsides, a large stone is all that reminds the passer-by that here a noble woman gave up her life rather than give up her Bible or assembling together with God's people. The influence of their noble lives is burnt into the Scottish character of to-day, and it is one of the proudest boasts of some Scotsmen that some of their female relatives shared in the sorrows and tribulations of the dark " killing time."

XII.

THE BAILLIES OF JERVISWOODE.

THE phrase " Baillies of Jerviswoode " recalls to the mind pleasant pictures of two persons famed for their goodness and greatness.

Robert Baillie was a noted man in his day, and his memory is sacred to every noble-hearted Scotsman. He was a great-grandson of the great reformer John Knox. Heredity may or may not count for much as far as character is concerned. This fact cannot be gainsaid: Baillie had in his heart the best features of the character of John Knox. " You have truly men of great spirits in Scotland," said Dr John Owen ; " there is, for a gentleman, Mr Baillie of Jerviswoode, a person of the greatest abilities I ever almost met with." " A gentleman of great parts," says Bishop Burnet, " but of much greater virtue."

Baillie was a Covenanter, and being such was debarred from taking public office. He was nevertheless a deep student of politics, and gradually became the real leader of all parties in England, Scotland, and Holland interested in the Covenanters.

" As for my principles in relation to government," he writes in one of his papers, " they are such as I ought not to be ashamed of, being consonant to the Word of

God, the Confession of Faith of the Reformed Churches, the rules of policy, reason, and humanity."

Although Baillie took little part in affairs publicly, yet the Government had far too many spies not to know the great position of influence Baillie had obtained in the councils of the Covenanters. When the "Rye House Plot" failed, as Baillie was a well-known friend of those who took part in that project, he was arrested.

The Duke of York conducted the examination himself in his usual coarse and brutal manner. Baillie knew nothing, and could tell nothing. This did not satisfy the King, who threatened Baillie with torture. He was sent back to prison and heavily ladened with chains, which completely broke down his constitution.

Seeing the distressful position of Baillie, the King offered him his liberty if he would give evidence against Lord William Russell. Even if Baillie could have done so, the bribe of his liberty would not have made him do this. The King coaxed and threatened; Baillie remained mute. And as they had no laws in England to condemn Baillie, he was sent down to Scotland and charged with treason.

Shut up in Edinburgh prison, although in a critical state of health, his wife was denied admittance to him. She even offered to be put in irons at his side to prevent any attempt at escape. This was refused.

It was the fear that they were to be robbed of the pleasure (!) of seeing him hung that caused them to relent. Baillie was sinking so fast they requested his wife to come and attend to him. Even then they were not sure but what he might die and cheat them, so they fined him £18,000, without trial, for entertaining Covenanters.

"Yet," says Burnet, "he was so composed, and even so cheerful, that his behaviour looked like the reviving of the spirit of the noblest of the old Greeks or Romans

ROBERT BAILLIE OF JERVISWOODE.

or rather of the primitive Christians and first martyrs, in those best days of the Church."

Men were put to the torture, and the evidence so given was used against Baillie. Some of his friends, to save their head, gave evidence against him. His confidential chats were sworn to as his public utterances. In this way they weaved a web to entangle him.

He was so weak that he was brought to the court in his dressing-gown. Lady Graden sat by his side, giving him every comfort possible. The evidence was given, and Sir George Mackenzie used all his powers to make a verdict of death certain.

Rising from his seat, Baillie tried to address the court.

" My Lord President, I desire liberty to speak a few words, not being able to say much because of my great weakness.

" My Lord, the sickness now upon me, in all human appearance, will soon prove mortal, and I cannot live many days. I find I am intended for a public sacrifice in life and estate, and my doom being predetermined, I am only sorry, under such circumstances, that my trial has given the court so much and so long trouble by staying here till past midnight.

" I have just one word to say to you, gentlemen," turning to the jury. " I doubt not but you will act as men of honour on the evidence which you have heard. The depositions of the witnesses, I admit, contain some hard things against me, and these must be your rule in coming to a verdict, and nothing that I can say may be entitled to any legal effect ; yet, for the exoneration of my own conscience, and that my poor memory and ruined family may not suffer additional injustice from the breath of calumny, I am bound to direct your attention to this, that the most material witnesses were former associates and correspondents of my own, connected in what I was connected, embarked in the same principles and cause. Life may be precious to them, and the saving of it may colour, or even add something to their evidence. One of them is certainly blessed with a very ready memory, which is never at a loss; yet I am sure there were some things said to have been spoken at a meeting at which I attended, which I am positive were not, at least not when I was present. As to the witnesses who have appeared against me, I do most heartily forgive them. There is one thing that distresses me extremely, and where I am injured to the last degree—that is, to be charged with a plot to cut off the King and the Duke of York; and that I was engaged in this with such an ardent zeal and fury that I sat up whole nights to form a declaration to palliate or justify such villainy. I am in all probability to appear in a few hours before the tribunal of the Great Judge. In His omniscient presence, and before your Lordships and all present, I solemnly declare that never was I prompted or privy to any such thing, and that I abhor and detest all thoughts or principles that would lead to touching the life and blood of his Majesty or his royal brother, or any person whatever."

There was only one word more he wished to say before his strength deserted him. He turned to the Lord Advocate, and addressed him:

" I think it strange beyond expression that you charge me with such abominable things. Do you remember, when you came to me in prison, you told me such things were laid to my charge, but you did not believe them? How then, my Lord, dare you throw a stain upon my character, and with so much violence of accusation?

Are you now convinced in your conscience that I am more guilty than I was at the interview where you freely acquitted me of guilt ?   Do you remember what passed betwixt us in prison ? "

The Lord Advocate cowed before these scathing words, and in an excited manner answered:

" Jerviswoode, I own what you say ; my thoughts there were as a private man.   What I say here is by special direction of the Privy Council. *He* knows my orders," pointing to Sir William Paterson, the clerk.

" Well, my Lord," said Baillie, with the utmost loathing and contempt, " if you keep one conscience for yourself and another for the Council, I pray God to forgive you—I do."

The whole of this speech was not for his own sake. He knew his doom was sealed, and the warrant signed before he came into court. Baillie's aim was to save his family as much as possible. The moment he sat down the jury gave in their verdict, and Jerviswoode was condemned to death.

" My Lords, the time is short, the sentence is sharp ; but I thank God, who hath made me as fit to die as you are to live."

He was hanged on the 21st December in the Market Cross of Edinburgh.   His head was put upon the Nether Bow.   His body was quartered, and sent to Jedburgh, Lanark, Ayr, Glasgow.

After his death, his wife and son George retired to Holland.   It was here George renewed his acquaintance with the daughter of Sir Patrick Hume, named Grisell, who became his wife.   She it was who added to the glory, already great, of the Baillies of Jerviswoode.

Grisell was brought up under the tuition of a noble and patriotic father. Sir Patrick took the side of the Covenanters, and in protesting on behalf of the shire of the Merse against certain hardships, he was imprisoned by the Court of Session. He was sent to Stirling, where he remained for several months before the King released him. On his release he was forbidden to hold any position of trust, by order of the King, dated February 24, 1676.

He was only allowed his liberty eighteen months, when he was again arrested. No charge was preferred against him. His health breaking down, he was transferred to Dumbarton Castle, where he lay for a year. Through the efforts of the Countess of Northumberland, the King granted Hume's release. It was then the reason of his arrest was given. "That he had been imprisoned for reasons known to the King and tending to secure the public peace."

During that year's imprisonment Grisell repeatedly went to see her father, although but a child. Lady Hume, through the cares of the home, and to avoid suspicion, never went to see her husband. Had she done so, she would not have been admitted. The governor of the castle saw no harm in admitting the young girl to see Sir Patrick.

When he returned home, the arrest of Robert Baillie, his intimate friend, took place. Sir Patrick feared he would be re-arrested, and determined to use every means available to escape. He lived in his house quietly for several months, when they were alarmed by the sight of dragoons coming to the house. Twice they came, but failed to find Sir Patrick.

K

The care of her father was in the hands of Grisell.
It was difficult to find a suitable place to hide him,
but after some search, the family vault at Polwarth
church was chosen. This was about a mile from the
house. It was a gruesome place, but all the safer through
this very fact.

Grisell wished a bed carried there, and had to make
one of the servants aware of Sir Patrick's hiding-place.
This man carried, bit by bit, a bed to the vault, and
Grisell brought clothes. For a whole month Sir Patrick
lived there, the only light being a small grating at one
of the vaults.

When all the house was asleep, Grisell stole out, and
although naturally timid, she walked through the churchyard and entered the dark vault. Whilst her father
partook of the food provided, Grisell told him all the
news. She stayed with him until the signs of the morning's light made her anxious to get home.

The difficulty of getting food for her father without
the servants suspecting anything was very great. Her
father was very fond of the plain Scotch dish—sheep's
head. Whilst the children were busy with their soup,
Grisell managed to slip into a table napkin a large piece
of a sheep's head, which was for dinner. One of the
children looked at the plate where the sheep's head had
been, and exclaimed: " Mother, will you look at Grisell;
while we have been eating our broth she has eaten up the
whole sheep's head!"

Grisell was anxious to get a place in the house to hide
her father, and chose a room on the ground floor. It
was her plan to make a bed for him under the floor.
With the assistance of the servant referred to before,

they lifted the floor and began to dig out the earth. *They scraped out the earth with their nails,* so afraid were they to arouse suspicion. Before it was accomplished Grisell's fingers were nailless, and torn and bleeding. The earth she took in a sheet and threw it out a top window, that the wind might well scatter it. Into the hole made they put a box, and Grisell's heart was filled with joy. When she came to view the box next day, it *was full of water !* Her last resort had failed. Perhaps it was as well, for soldiers were constantly prowling about.

It was the news of the execution of Robert Baillie of Jerviswoode that determined Sir Patrick to go to Holland. Grisell made garments to disguise her father, and he started off like some broken-down doctor.

He was not out of the way a day too soon. Proceedings had been taken against him for treason—a charge as false as any could be. His goods were ordered to be delivered to the King. Soon after this her mother went to London. The object of Lady Hume was to get out of the estate her marriage jointure. In this she succeeded so far, obtaining £150 a year. They then went to Holland.

Grisell became the servant of the family, and the personal attendant on her father. She was so gentle of heart, upright in spirit, yet so meek and full of love, she seemed willing to bless everybody. Twice she had gone over to Scotland on business for her father, her natural shrewdness making her surmount all difficulties in such a perilous undertaking.

Her brother joined the Prince of Orange's guards, and found George Baillie a soldier there. Soon they were promoted to positions worthy of their rank and character.

Baillie became a constant visitor at Sir Patrick's house.
It was a joy to everyone when Grisell became the accepted
lover of George Baillie.

The Prince of Orange took Sir Patrick into his counsel,
and Sir Patrick, his son, and George Baillie came over to
England with the Prince. The success that followed
that coming over filled the heart of Britain with joy.
Grisell was attached to the Princess of Orange, and in
due time came over to this country with her.

It was one of the first concerns of the Prince of Orange
to restore the estates of Baillie and Sir Patrick Hume to
their rightful owners. George Baillie at once pressed
Grisell to become his wife, and the union took place at
her father's house on September 17, 1692.

In the combination of these two families the name of
Jerviswoode was once more brought to the front.

The nobility of Grisell is best testified to in the words
of her mother and daughter.

" My dear Grisell, blessed be you above all, for a helpful
child have you been to me," said her mother.

" None could better judge," says her daughter, " than
herself what was most proper to be done upon any
occasion ; of which my father was so convinced, that I
have good reason to believe he never did anything of
consequence through his whole life without asking her
advice."

It is pleasant to record that after all Sir Patrick had
suffered, he became one of the King's Privy Councillors.
Although Robert Baillie had sealed his testimony with
his blood, his son lived to enjoy peace and happiness in
a time when what his father pleaded for and died for
was carried out.

XIII.

LADY CALDWELL.

It is to the honour of the wealthy classes that they took a prominent share in the carrying out of the Reformation in Scotland. The Covenanters had in their midst the pick of the land in wealth, learning, and piety. This may have arisen largely from the fact, that the Covenanting struggle was supported by the most noble and holy women of Scotland. No persecution could alter their allegiance; and the story of their sufferings and woes is a very sad one indeed. The story of Lady Caldwell will bear me out in this.

A Barbara Cunningham was married in 1657 to William Muir of Caldwell. By a custom of the age she was called Lady Caldwell.

Mr Muir was a strong Covenanter. He had raised a troop of fifty horses to join the Pentland rising, but hearing that General Dalziel was to prevent his joining the Covenanters, Muir disbanded his company. After the disaster of Pentland, Muir knew his life was in danger, and fled to Holland.

He was charged with treason, and, as he did not appear, his lands, goods, dignities, and all things whatsoever were forfeited for the use of the King. A man was appointed to collect the rents, and the estate was passed over to General Dalziel.

Lady Caldwell was now left penniless. Although allowed to live in the house, the cattle were taken away, the rents were arrested, the movable things sold. Her estimate of what she lost in three years was £8000.

Having no special reason for staying in Scotland, she now went to Holland and joined her husband. They became highly respected, so that Robert M'Ward said, " As a companion we had but one Caldwell amongst all the gentlemen I knew or yet know in Scotland. His wife did also cheerfully choose to be his fellow-exile and companion in tribulation, as she desired to be in the kingdom and patience of Jesus Christ."

Lady Caldwell's troubles were much increased by the death of her husband. She then returned to Scotland, and finding her house unoccupied she partly furnished it and abode there. General Dalziel evicted her and her four children, and took her furniture. Friends offered her money, but she preferred to work for the necessaries of life, and did so, living in a small house in Glasgow. It was a great change for her, who had been accustomed to every luxury, but she never repined. For twelve years she lived in quietness, blessed by the devotion of her children, and the peace of God abiding upon her.

And one morning she was arrested and sent to one of the state prisons without trial or indictment. When she questioned the jailers why she was imprisoned, they replied that she had been entertaining outlawed ministers. Her eldest daughter, Jean, was next arrested, and the two were taken to the castle of Blackness. Here Lady Caldwell was a prisoner for three years, her daughter for six months.

Various appeals to the Privy Council were made by

Lady Caldwell. In reply to these she was allowed to walk in the castle courtyard! When her daughter Anne lay sick of fever, two miles from Blackness, she requested as a favour to be allowed to see her " dearly beloved dying daughter." She agreed to go in chains; but under no condition was she permitted. Her daughter died and was buried within a mile of her mother. This was a terrible trial to Lady Caldwell, and is only one of the ways in which she was tortured in prison.

At the end of three years she was liberated and joined her children. The rest of her days were spent in peace. When the Revolution took place all her husband's lands and honours were restored to her by Act of Parliament.

XIV.

SOME WONDERFUL ESCAPES.

IT has evoked surprise in the hearts of many that, during the fifty years the Covenanting struggle endured, so few were put to death. These men value life at a small price. Eighteen thousand lives were sacrificed, at least, and the reason the number was not greater is due to the wonderful escapes many had.

There is a story told of two Covenanters who were hunted by dragoons from the wilds of Carsphairn. They determined to cross the River Nith for safety. To their amazement, as they ascended the opposite bank, they came in full view of the curate playing quoits on the green. They instantly gave up themselves as lost. The curate, however, had compassion upon the poor hunted men.

" Doff your coats, and come and play a game with me," cried the curate. This they readily consented to do, and were delighted to see the dragoons ride past the manse in great haste. This gives an illustration of the kindly feeling *some*—very few though—had for the poor Covenanters.

They often escaped from death through one of the dragoons really being a Covenanter in disguise.

On the banks of the Carple Burn, which discharges

itself into the Nith, the Covenanters often found shelter in the overhanging bank. This became known to the sergeant of a company of dragoons, and search was to be made next day. One of the dragoons knew where a man was hiding, and, detaching himself from the rest the evening before the search, went to where this man lay.

" Oh, true," said the dragoon, " if you know where there are any of the hill-folk hiding in this glen, tell them from me the dragoons are going to search this glen to-morrow." It is needless to say this advice did not require repeating. The dragoons found everything but Covenanters in that glen.

Some of them were near captured, but escaped. In a farm-house near Eliock, several of the hill-folk were enjoying a good breakfast, kindly provided by the generous farmer. As they sat at food a company of dragoons rode up to the door.

" Run into the barn and hide amongst the corn sheaves," cried the farmer; at the same time hiding everything that would create suspicion.

" We have come to buy some corn, good sir," said the corporal in charge. " We hear you have some good stuff to sell."

" Yes, 'tis better this year than others." And he led them to the barn.

The Covenanters lay in terrible fear as they heard the dragoons enter the barn. The farmer soon spoke in such a manner, that they knew there was little danger if they only kept quiet. They were exceedingly glad to hear the corporal say, " I think we have enough now." The Covenanters finished their breakfast in peace and thankfulness.

The escape, however, was not always so easily accomplished.

At a place near Sanquhar lived a man named Hair, well known for his godly life. The dragoons caught him and doomed him to death, and determined his death should give them some sport. They placed him on horseback and rode to a hill which stands above Glen Aylmer. The descent into the glen is very steep, in some places almost perpendicular. It was the intention of the dragoons to shoot Hair, and let his body roll down the steep mountain side. In climbing the hill, however, his feet had become unbound. As the soldiers unbound Hair, the prisoner, like a flash of light, slid from the horse and jumped over the terrible hillside. He slid down with great speed towards Glen Aylmer, catching bushes and heather as he went along. The dragoons fired at him, but he was not hit. To the amazement of the dragoons, Hair was able to walk up the glen after such a terrible experience. Like many a one before and after him, he died in peace in bed.

An escape of a different character was that of Messrs Dun, Paterson, and Richard. They, and several others, had been in hiding, when a company of dragoons found them out. The three mentioned were taken prisoners, and marched across the hills to the dragoons' quarters. As they crossed the hills, however, the heavens grew black, and the air murky. A great flash of lightning lit up the heavens, and the thunder crashed as it only can on a hill-top. The horses of the dragoons reared and plunged. Flash succeeded flash, and the hills echoed and re-echoed the roar of the thunder. Hail came down fiercely, making the horses unmanageable. The leader fled as fast as he could to a farmhouse, regardless of his men and prisoners. The men became panic-stricken and followed his example, leaving the prisoners to escape. The storm was a messenger of life and peace to them, and they were deeply thankful to God for their timely escape.

Liberty and life, however, had often to be won before it was granted. This was true of Adam Clark of Glenim. He and about thirty others were enjoying breakfast in a hut on the hillside. Clark was surprised to see a sheep rush past the door, and dismayed when he saw a dog after it. He knew their place of hiding was known, and he instantly rushed into the hut and told his friends about their danger. They ran out to hide amongst the heather and bracken.

"Take Adam Clark if you take no one else," was the order the officer gave. Clark was soon attacked by a dragoon, but dismounted him and spared his life. He went to the rescue of his brother, Andrew, and by a deft use of his sword, wrested the dragoon's sword out of his hand. He then rushed down the deep gully the Nith torrent had made, and thus escaped.

Adam Clark once again had to fight for his life. He had gone to the home of a sympathiser for food, and whilst there the house was surrounded.

"You are all my prisoners" cried the sergeant gaily, and prepared ropes to tie the prisoners' hands behind their backs.

Clark and his companion were not to be taken without a fight. The two boldly went to the door and defied the dragoons. Before the leader could give orders, Clark and his companion had passed through the dragoons, and were soon out of sight.

Andrew Clark was once met by Colonel James Douglas, and charged with injuring some dragoons. The charge was unfounded. Colonel Douglas, however, determined to shoot Clark, and told him to prepare to meet his God. Clark knelt down on the heather and prayed out of a full heart, specially mentioning the officer by name, and asking God to forgive the mistake he was making.

Before he had finished his prayer his old nurse came and pleaded to the Colonel.

" Halt there, for it will be an ill thing if an innocent man's blood is shed this day. Andrew never did that of which you charge him. My husband fought at the side of your honoured uncle, sir, and for his sake I claim the life of this man, for whom I entertain a mother's affection."

After some explanations Clark's life was spared.

Some of the means adopted to escape were slightly humourous. Some Covenanters were in hiding at Auchengrouch, when they saw some dragoons making to the farmhouse where they were hiding. The mistress of the farm was a clever-witted woman.

" Come up here and dress in some of my clothes. You will act as servants."

As the dragoons came to the farmhouse door, they heard the mistress scolding the servants for their clumsiness. The soldiers were amused at the shame-facedness of the servants, and after a look round, departed.

The rescue in the Enterkin Pass caused consternation in Edinburgh, and rejoicing in the midst of the Covenanters, and deserves a place in this chapter.

James Harkness, of Lockerben, hearing that a company of soldiers were taking a number of Covenanters to Edinburgh, determined to organise a rescue party. The spot of rescue chosen was the Enterkin Pass, a narrow valley through which a turbulent stream runs, with high hills on either side. The path through this valley is on the face of the south hill. It was arranged to dig out a trench on the north hill, and then to fire upon the dragoons, if necessary, from this place of vantage.

The soldiers and prisoners came marching along, and soon were hailed by James Harkness. The answer given was the rattling of bullets on the hillside. One of the friends of Harkness taking deadly aim, killed the commander. The soldiers then became demoralised and allowed the Covenanters to go free.

Children were not beneath the fury of the dragoons; and many a young life was sacrificed on the hillside. Many had wonderful escapes, however. John M'Call, of Dalzien, was at a meeting where some Covenanters were shot. He was ordered by the captain to go to the river for water to wash away the blood stains on the officer's hands. The boy, however, rushed off, and began to climb the hill. The soldiers fired upon him, but, being fleet of foot, he escaped.

There is a story told of James Murray, of Ashiestiel, who was being threatened by the soldiers.

" Unless you tell me where the meeting is held you shall be shot," said the sergeant. The boy agreed to take the officer where the meeting was held, knowing well that the people had by that time gone home. Whilst carrying the sergeant over the Tweed, James threw him over his head into the river, and dived into a

deep hole himself. The soldiers laughed at the drenched
appearance of their leader. Search was made for the
boy, but he could not be found. He had hidden amidst
the willows at the edge of the water.

Some Covenanters escaped in a very simple manner.
Kent was a preacher who had to flee for his life from
one place to another. He was found fishing one day by
a company of soldiers.

"That is our man, for he has a set of teeth like Kent."
This was greeted with a burst of derisive laughter.

"If this were Kent, he would not be fishing, but praying and preaching." And with this the soldiers turned
away.

The wit of Michael Smith, of Quarrelwood, was the
means of saving two Covenanters who had come to
house for food and shelter. As they were sitting by the
fire, a party of dragoons galloped to the door.

"I doubt but that we are lost men, Michael."

"Not so fast, my friends. Here you must appear to
have been inspecting this malt, and have fallen asleep
over it." He accordingly spread out the malt, and they
laid their heads on their hands.

"Have you any Covenanters here?" asked the leader
of the dragoons.

"Yea, come in and see two worthy Covenanters I
have here. They are worthy of such a great cause," he
said with a burst of laughter. When the dragoons
entered the room and saw the two men apparently
asleep, drunk, they laughed heartily at what they
thought was a joke of Smith's.

John Colvin, of Dormont, was eagerly sought for by the
dragoons. They came one evening, and Colvin rushed

behind the bed for safety. In came the bustling dragoons, and began to search for Colvin. They searched in vain. They now began to ill-treat Mrs Colvin and her little child. The screams of his wife and child roused Colvin's anger, and he crept from under the bed, and rushed at a dragoon who was ill-treating his wife. He was soon overpowered and dragged along the floor. His wife had meanwhile escaped, and went screaming down the hillside. She was met by a company of Covenanters who were wandering about. She told her story, and with a shout of anger they entered the house. The soldiers put out the light, and got out of the house as fast as they could, glad to make their escape. Colvin was soon released, and laughed heartily at the discomfiture of the dragoons.

Andrew Forsyth, of Kirkcowan, had gone home to bid his family farewell before going south out of danger. He was holding devotional talk with his family when some troops rode up to the door. One or two entered, and laying hands on Andrew, said .

" Are you the Galloway drover ? "

" I am a shepherd, not a drover."

" I see you are the man we want, at any rate, so come along."

They put him on horseback, and tied his feet under the belly of the horse. A soldier rode in front of him. The company then started along the hillside, which was very full of bogs.

Gradually the horse with the double burden got behind the others. It was a dark, misty night, and great care had to be taken in going along. The horse frequently stumbled, and at last fell. The fall threw the soldier forward and stunned him, and at the same time released Andrew's legs. He immediately ran up the hill, and escaped. The other soldiers missed their companion and came back to his help, only to find the prisoner out of sight.

Thus another life was spared to thank God for protection, and to glorify Him by his life.

THE END.